Hyper-V Security

Secure your Hyper-V hosts, their guests, and critical services from intruders and malware

Eric Siron

Andy Syrewicze

PUBLISHING

BIRMINGHAM - MUMBAI

Hyper-V Security

First published: December 2014

Production reference: 1191214

Published by Packt Publishing Ltd.
Livery Place
35 Livery Street
Birmingham B3 2PB, UK.

ISBN 978-1-78217-549-0

www.packtpub.com

Credits

Authors
Eric Siron

Andy Syrewicze

Reviewers
Daniel Clarke

Milton Goh

Eric Mann

Lai Yoong Seng

Acquisition Editor
Sam Wood

Content Development Editor
Arwa Manasawala

Technical Editors
Shiny Poojary

Sebastian Rodrigues

Copy Editors
Pranjali Chury

Alfida Paiva

Project Coordinator
Danuta Jones

Proofreaders
Simran Bhogal

Maria Gould

Ameesha Green

Indexer
Tejal Soni

Graphics
Abhinash Sahu

Production Coordinator
Aparna Bhagat

Cover Work
Aparna Bhagat

About the Authors

Eric Siron has over 15 years of professional experience in the information technology field. He has architected solutions across the spectrum, from two-user home offices to thousand-user enterprises. He began working with Microsoft Hyper-V Server in 2010, and has focused on Microsoft Virtualization technologies ever since. He is currently employed as a senior system administrator at The University of Iowa Hospitals and Clinics in Iowa City, Iowa. He is a regular contributor to the Hyper-V Portal blog hosted by Altaro Software. In addition to this book, he is the author of *Microsoft Hyper-V Cluster Design, Packt Publishing,* and the creator of the screencast series, *Building and Managing a Virtual Environment with Hyper-V Server 2012 R2, Packt Publishing.*

My work in this book is dedicated to my wife and daughter, who sacrificed so much of their time while I was writing it. Thanks to my co-author Andrew Syrewicze for juggling this in his busy schedule. Very special thanks to Ulrike Carlson for rushing to the aid of an author in distress.

Andy Syrewicze has spent the last 11 years and more in providing technology solutions across several industry verticals, including education, healthcare, and professional services, and Fortune 500 manufacturing companies. His skills include VMware, Linux, and Network Security, but his focus over the last 7 years has been on Virtualization, Cloud Services, and the Microsoft Server Stack, with a focus on Hyper-V. That said, he has become quite involved in the Microsoft IT community over the last 2 years via a number of different mediums, such as various blogs, IT boot camps, and podcasts. He has also been named an MVP by Microsoft specifically for his contributions to the Hyper-V community. He has been featured as a co-host of the Technet Radio shows *Hyper-V from a VMware Admin's Perspective* and *Building your Hybrid Cloud*, which have been syndicated on Microsoft's `channel9.msdn.com` website. His other notable skills are professional blogging and public speaking, both of which he participates in on a regular basis. He has a passion for technology, and greatly enjoys sharing his knowledge with peers, customers, and the IT community at large.

I would first like to thank my wife, son, and family, for always inspiring me to be better than what I am. I would also like to thank my co-author Eric for giving me the opportunity to work on this project, and the team at Packt Publishing, for their continuous patience with my (at times) crazy schedule.

About the Reviewers

Daniel Clarke has worked in the IT field for more than 10 years, thereby working with various Microsoft products with a specialization in Hyper-V and System Center Virtual Machine Manager. He has designed and implemented several Microsoft Virtualization platforms, two of which have been recognized with the Management & Virtualization Partner of the Year (2012 and 2013) and Server Platform Partner of the Year (2013) awards by Microsoft, New Zealand. He currently works in New Zealand as a senior infrastructure consultant. His previous roles include that of a consulting engineer, acting as a Tech Lead for a Managed Services department, and various Systems Engineer and support-based roles. His primary work these days usually involves Hyper-V and the System Center Suite, primarily Virtual Machine Manager, Operations Manager, and Orchestrator.

I would like to thank Laura for always encouraging me and supporting me through my career.

Milton Goh started out in the IT industry in 2005, where he began as a software developer, meddling with various programming languages that range from Visual Basic to Visual C#. He has always focused on the Microsoft suite of products and technologies, and is an avid fan of Microsoft technologies. Since the start of his career, he has ventured into different roles within the industry, ranging from a developer and consultant to an architect, where he helps to resolve the pain points of his clients. He is one of the leaders for the Singapore PowerShell User Group community, where he plays an important role of spreading the word about PowerShell to everyone. He possesses a strong will to evangelize PowerShell technologies to IT professionals and developers in the industry. He spends his free time meddling with various technologies in his home lab or the lab that is built on Microsoft Azure. This is the second Hyper-V book that he has reviewed for Packt Publishing; his first book was *Hyper-V Replica Essentials*.

> I would like to thank the team at Packt Publishing for choosing me again as a technical reviewer, which forces me to relook at the technical details that various authors have written. No one is perfect in this world; everyone is bound to make mistakes in life. Therefore, it is definitely a learning opportunity to be able to refresh my knowledge that I gained over the years in the industry. I would like to thank my family and my girlfriend Cindy Askara for being there in my life, supporting me while I was being a nerd, and spending most of my time on technical stuff.

Eric Mann is a seasoned web developer with experience in languages ranging from JavaScript and Ruby to C#. He has been building websites of all shapes and sizes for the better part of a decade and continues to experiment with new technologies and techniques. Eric is a senior web engineer at 10up (http://10up.com), where he focuses on developing high-end web solutions powered by WordPress. He also blogs frequently on software techniques, security, and development practices at https://eamann.com.

Lai Yoong Seng was awarded Microsoft Most Valuable Professional (MVP) in Hyper-V in 2010. He has more than 14 years of IT experience, and recently joined Hyper-V and System Center Specialist Infront Consulting in Malaysia. He specializes in Microsoft Virtualization, and has started blogging (`www.ms4u.info`) and presenting for local and regional events. He is the founder of Malaysia Virtualization User Group (MVUG), which provides a one-stop center for people to learn about Hyper-V, System Center, and Azure. Previously, he was actively engaged as a Technology Early Adopter (TAP) and a tester for System Center Virtual Machine Manager 2012, System Center 2012 SP1, Windows Server 2012 R2, System Center 2012 R2, and Azure Site Recovery. He was a technical reviewer for *Windows Server 2012 Hyper-V: Deploying Hyper-V Enterprise Server Virtualization Platform*, *Packt Publishing*, *Hyper-V Network Virtualization Cookbook*, *Packt Publishing* and for the video *Building and Managing a Virtual Environment with Hyper-V Server 2012 R2*, *Packt Publishing*.

Reviewing a book takes a lot of effort and is a difficult process. It would not have been possible without help from family, colleagues, and friends. I would like to thank my parents for being understanding and patient, and helping to keep all the other stuff together while I was reviewing a book. In addition, a very special thanks to Packt Publishing for giving me the opportunity to contribute to this book.

www.PacktPub.com

Support files, eBooks, discount offers, and more

For support files and downloads related to your book, please visit www.PacktPub.com.

Did you know that Packt offers eBook versions of every book published, with PDF and ePub files available? You can upgrade to the eBook version at www.PacktPub.com and as a print book customer, you are entitled to a discount on the eBook copy. Get in touch with us at service@packtpub.com for more details.

At www.PacktPub.com, you can also read a collection of free technical articles, sign up for a range of free newsletters and receive exclusive discounts and offers on Packt books and eBooks.

https://www2.packtpub.com/books/subscription/packtlib

Do you need instant solutions to your IT questions? PacktLib is Packt's online digital book library. Here, you can search, access, and read Packt's entire library of books.

Why subscribe?

- Fully searchable across every book published by Packt
- Copy and paste, print, and bookmark content
- On demand and accessible via a web browser

Free access for Packt account holders

If you have an account with Packt at www.PacktPub.com, you can use this to access PacktLib today and view 9 entirely free books. Simply use your login credentials for immediate access.

Instant updates on new Packt books

Get notified! Find out when new books are published by following @PacktEnterprise on Twitter or the *Packt Enterprise* Facebook page.

Table of Contents

Preface

The reality of computing in today's world is that nothing is safe. Securing a network of computer systems is a never-ending quest that involves constant vigilance. The explosion of virtualization technologies has introduced a new set of complexities for administrators to master. This book's purpose is to navigate through the tools available to lock down your Hyper-V environment. It includes high-level examinations of concepts as well as practical guidance for implementation.

What this book covers

Chapter 1, Introducing Hyper-V Security, starts by discussing the important concepts of security in a Hyper-V environment.

Chapter 2, Securing the Host, deals with securing the management operating system. A Hyper-V system runs a critical hypervisor, but it also runs a server operating system that has its own security requirements.

Chapter 3, Securing Virtual Machines from the Hypervisor, focuses on Hyper-V security from the perspective of the hypervisor.

Chapter 4, Securing Virtual Machines, turns the attention from the hypervisor to its guests. This includes not only securing them as virtual machines, but as computers that run typical operating systems and applications with security needs of their own.

Chapter 5, Securing the Network, covers a variety of methods that are at your disposal to secure network communications for both hosts and guests.

Chapter 6, Securing Hyper-V Storage, details the considerations and techniques involved for the protection of your virtual machines' data.

Chapter 7, Hyper-V Security and System Center VMM, explores System Center Virtual Machine Manager and discusses how having SCVMM in play changes the security discussion.

Chapter 8, Secure Hybrid Cloud Management through App Controller, discusses system requirements, installation, and configuration of App Controller, including its role-based security model for multiple public/private clouds.

What you need for this book

For the first six chapters of this book, you will need one system that runs Windows Server or Hyper-V Server Version 2012 or later. If you're using Hyper-V Server, you'll need a second computer that runs the same level of Windows Server or a Professional or Enterprise edition of Windows in order to follow along using graphical tools. PowerShell alternatives have been provided, so this graphical system is not strictly necessary.

Who this book is for

This book is intended for administrators who are experienced with Windows Server, Active Directory, and Hyper-V. It does not cover installation or basic operations of any of these technologies. Where possible, references to external information sources have been provided.

Conventions

In this book, you will find a number of styles of text that distinguish between different kinds of information. Here are some examples of these styles, and an explanation of their meaning.

Code words in text, database table names, folder names, filenames, file extensions, pathnames, dummy URLs, user input, and Twitter handles are shown as follows: "The cmdlet to check the installation status of items is Get-WindowsFeature."

A block of code is set as follows:

```
$TargetSystems = "svhv1", "svhv2"
$ScriptBlock = {
  $StoppedStates = "Off", "Saved"
  $StoppedVMs = Get-VM | where { $_.State -in $StoppedStates }
  $StoppedVMs | Start-VM
  $StoppedVMs | select Name
}
```

Any command-line input or output is written as follows:

```
certutil -viewstore My
certutil -viewstore Root
```

New terms and **important words** are shown in bold. Words that you see on the screen, in menus or dialog boxes for example, appear in the text like this: "Turn it off on the **Features** page of the **Add Roles and Features** wizard in Server Manager."

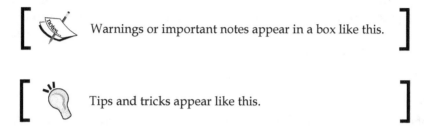

Warnings or important notes appear in a box like this.

Tips and tricks appear like this.

Reader feedback

Feedback from our readers is always welcome. Let us know what you think about this book—what you liked or may have disliked. Reader feedback is important for us to develop titles that you really get the most out of.

To send us general feedback, simply send an e-mail to feedback@packtpub.com, and mention the book title via the subject of your message.

If there is a topic that you have expertise in and you are interested in either writing or contributing to a book, see our author guide on www.packtpub.com/authors.

Customer support

Now that you are the proud owner of a Packt book, we have a number of things to help you to get the most from your purchase.

Downloading the example code

You can download the example code files for all Packt books you have purchased from your account at http://www.packtpub.com. If you purchased this book elsewhere, you can visit http://www.packtpub.com/support and register to have the files e-mailed directly to you.

Errata

Although we have taken every care to ensure the accuracy of our content, mistakes do happen. If you find a mistake in one of our books—maybe a mistake in the text or the code—we would be grateful if you would report this to us. By doing so, you can save other readers from frustration and help us improve subsequent versions of this book. If you find any errata, please report them by visiting http://www.packtpub.com/submit-errata, selecting your book, clicking on the **errata submission form** link, and entering the details of your errata. Once your errata are verified, your submission will be accepted and the errata will be uploaded on our website, or added to any list of existing errata, under the Errata section of that title. Any existing errata can be viewed by selecting your title from http://www.packtpub.com/support.

Piracy

Piracy of copyright material on the Internet is an ongoing problem across all media. At Packt, we take the protection of our copyright and licenses very seriously. If you come across any illegal copies of our works, in any form, on the Internet, please provide us with the location address or website name immediately so that we can pursue a remedy.

Please contact us at copyright@packtpub.com with a link to the suspected pirated material.

We appreciate your help in protecting our authors, and our ability to bring you valuable content.

Questions

You can contact us at questions@packtpub.com if you are having a problem with any aspect of the book, and we will do our best to address it.

Introducing Hyper-V Security

1

One of the most difficult tribulations in the entire realm of computing is security. Computers are tools, and just like any tool, they are designed to be used. Unfortunately, not every usage is proper, and not every computer should be accessed by just anyone. A computer really has no way to classify proper usage against improper usage, or differentiate between a valid user and an unauthorized user any more than a hammer would. The act of securing them is quite literally an endeavor to turn them against their purpose.

Hyper-V adds new dimensions to the security problem. Virtual machines have protection options that mirror their physical counterparts, but present unique challenges. The hypervisor presents challenges of its own, both in its role as the host for those virtual machines and through the management operating system that manifests it.

In this chapter, we'll cover:

- The importance of Hyper-V security
- Basic security concerns
- A starting point to security
- The terminology of Hyper-V
- Acquiring Hyper-V

The importance of Hyper-V security

For many, security seems like a blatantly obvious necessity. For others, the need isn't as clear. Many decision-makers don't believe that their organization's product requires in-depth protection. Many administrators believe that the default protections are sufficient. There are certainly some institutions whose needs don't require an elaborate regimen of protections, but no one can skip due diligence.

Your clients expect it

The exact definition of a "client" varies from organization to organization, but every organization type provides some sort of service to someone. Whether you are a retail outlet or a non-profit organization that provides intangible services to individuals in need that cannot pay for them, your institution has an implicit agreement to protect the information relevant to those who depend on you. They most likely won't have any idea what Hyper-V is or what you use it for, but they will know enough to be displeased if it is revealed that any of your computer systems are not secure. Your organization could be vulnerable to litigation if clients believe their data is not being treated with sufficient importance.

Your stakeholders expect it

As with clients, stakeholders can mean many things. Simplistically, it's anyone who has a "stake" in the well-being of your organization. This could be members of the board of directors who aren't privy to day-to-day operations. It could be external investors. It could even include the previously mentioned clients. Even if they have no way to understand what's necessary or unnecessary to secure, they expect that it's being handled. Furthermore, they may disagree with you on what data is important to protect. If it's later discovered that something wasn't fully guarded that they assumed was being treated as highly confidential, the response could have extremely negative consequences.

Your employees and volunteers expect it

Almost all organizations have digitized some vital information of its employees and volunteers. They expect that this data is held in the highest confidentiality and is well guarded against theft and espionage. Even if the rest of your institution's data requires no particular protection, personnel data must always be safeguarded. In many jurisdictions, this is a legal requirement. Even if you aren't under the rule of law, civil litigation is always a possibility.

Experience has taught us that security is important

In the past, it was believed that attackers came from outside the institution and were simply after quick and easy money sources, such as credit card numbers. However, reality has shown that breaches occur for a wide variety of reasons, and many aren't obvious until after it's too late to do anything about it. The next section, *Basic Security Concerns*, will highlight a number of both common and unexpected attack types.

Weak points aren't always obvious

You know that you need to protect access to sensitive backend data with frontend passwords. You know that information traveling between the two needs to be encrypted. However, are you aware of every single point that the data will travel through? Is the storage location unprotected? Has there been a recent audit of individuals with access? Is there another application on one of the component systems that allows for unencrypted communications or remote access? Treating any system as though it doesn't need to be secured could allow it to become a gateway for others.

The costs of repair exceeds the costs of prevention

The summary of this section's message is that failing to enact security measures is not an acceptable option. It's not unusual to find people who understand that security is important, but believe that it's simply too expensive and that the systems to be protected are just not worth the effort. In reality, the costs of a breach can be catastrophic. Just adding up the previous points can lead you to that conclusion. Between lawyer bills, court costs, and any awards, litigation costs can be unbearably high. Of course, a breach might directly result in a financial loss of some kind. Beyond that, a loss of trust inevitably follows the compromise of systems, and this can have a greater long-term impact than anything else. Even when all those problems are taken care of, it's still necessary to clean up any damage to the systems and close the exploited breach points.

Basic security concerns

With a topic as large as computer security, it's always tough to know where to start. The best place is generally to begin by getting an idea of where and what your largest risk factors are. Every organization will have its own specific areas of concern, but there are a number of common elements that everyone needs to worry about.

Attack motivations

To understand what risks you face, it helps to know the reasons for which you might find yourself under attack. For many malware generators, there isn't a lot of reason involved. They write destructive code because they like destruction; they might be working from a place of genuine malice or a simple disregard for the well-being of others. For many others, their work comes from a need for vengeance over a real or perceived slight. The trespasses they seek revenge for could be relatively petty things, but some attacks are carried out over much more serious events, even major political affairs. Some authors seek a degree of notoriety, perhaps not among the public at large as much as a small group or subculture.

Financial motivation can be the source of both the most benign and the most dangerous security compromise. For instance, someone may want to prove eligibility for a job by showing that they possess the necessary skills to secure a system. One possible way is by demonstrating an ability to compromise that system. Such breaches generally require a deep understanding of the relevant technology, so they can effectively illustrate thorough knowledge. As long as these examples are never released "into the wild" and are instead disclosed to the system manufacturer so that a fix can be engineered, they are ultimately harmless. Unfortunately, a great many attackers seek a shorter-term gain through methods such as extortion from the manufacturer or owners of compromised systems or theft of sensitive data.

Data theft is often thought of in terms of financial information, such as credit card data. However, intellectual property should also be kept heavily guarded. Data that seems relatively benign might also be a target; if an attacker discovers that your company uses a specific e-mail template and can also obtain a list of customer e-mail accounts; they have enough information to launch a very convincing phishing campaign.

Untargeted attacks

The untargeted attack is likely the most common of all attacks, and can be the most disruptive. These generally manifest as viruses and worms. In the earlier days of computing, the most common distribution methods were, surprisingly, media that had been created by software makers for distribution of applications. Someone would modify the image data during the duplication process and ship malware to customers.

As the Internet rose in popularity, it introduced new ways for malware to make the rounds. First came e-mail. Next, websites became pick-up locations for all types of malicious software. New technologies that allowed for enhanced interactivity and the embedding of rich media, such as JavaScript and Adobe's (originally Shockwave's) Flash, were also used as vehicles for destructive software.

Most of the early malware was simply destructive. It wreaked havoc on data, corrupted systems, and locked users out of their own hardware. Later, they became money-making avenues for the unscrupulous. An example is **key loggers**, which capture key presses and sometimes mouse movements and clicks in an attempt to compromise logins and other sensitive data, such as credit card numbers. Another much more recent introduction is **ransomware**, which encrypts or deletes information with a promise to restore the data on payment.

Some of the most surreptitious untargeted attacks are relatively low-tech. One such attack is called **phishing**. This involves using some form of convincing technique, usually through e-mail, to lure users into volunteering sensitive information.

An attack vector related to phishing is **spam** e-mail. Most people just consider spam to be annoying, untargeted e-mail advertisements, but results from an experiment conducted in 2008 by McAfee, Inc., called **Spammed Persistently All Month (SPAM)**, would seem to indicate that most spam also qualifies as a scam in some form or another.

Another untargeted attack vector is any connection that a computer system makes into a public network. In the modern era, this is generally through a system's entry point into the Internet. With a limited number of Internet-accessible IP addresses available, attackers can simply scan large ranges of them, seeking systems that respond. Using automated tools, they can attempt to break through any security barriers that are in place.

Untargeted attacks pose few risks that are specific to Hyper-V, so this book won't spend a great deal of time on that topic. While no defense can be perfect, they are generally mitigated effectively through standard practices.

Targeted attacks

The most common attacks are untargeted, but targeted attacks can be the most dangerous. These come in a variety of forms but often use similar techniques to untargeted attacks. One example would be a phishing e-mail that appears to have been sent from your internal IT department, asking you to confirm your user name and password. Another would be a website that looks like an internal corporate site, such as a payroll page, which captures your login information instead of displaying your latest pay stub.

Some targeted attacks work against an organization's exposed faces. An immediately recognizable example is online banking. Most banks provide some method for their customers to access their accounts online, and they almost invariably include powerful tools such as money transfer systems. Of course, theft isn't necessarily the goal of a target attack. One well-known activity is the **denial-of-service** attack, in which an immense number of bogus requests are sent to a target system in a short amount of time, causing its services to be unavailable to legitimate users.

The computing device

Most of the compromises you are likely to deal with occur at the level of the computing device. Some of the most complex software in use today is the operating system. With thousands of programmers working on millions of lines of code, much of it left over from previous versions and programmers, it's just an unavoidable fact that all major operating systems contain security flaws. With millions of people working to locate these holes, regardless of their intentions, it's equally inevitable that these faults will be discovered and they will be compromised.

The advent and rising popularity of smartphones and tablets has increased the number of potential attack sources. As more and more devices become "smart," such as common environmental controls and food storage equipment, they too introduce new entry points from which an entire network can be compromised.

The network

The true risk of the single compromised device is the network that it's attached to. By breaching the network itself, an attacker potentially gains the ability to eavesdrop on all communications or launch a direct attack against specific computers or groups of systems. Since many organizations consider some areas to be secured since they are behind measures such as firewalls, breaching the protecting devices exposes everything that they are intended to protect.

Data-processing points

Raw data is rarely useful to end users. There are many systems in place whose jobs are to sort, process, retrieve, and organize information, and they often use well-known techniques to do this. Anything that's well-known is open to assault. Common examples are SQL database servers, e-mail systems, content management applications, and customer relationship management software. When these systems are broken into, the data they work with is ripe for the taking.

Data storage

A lot of effort is poured into securing end points, processing systems, and networks, but a disturbingly high amount of data storage locations are left relatively unprotected. Many administrators simply believe that all paths to the storage are well protected, so the storage location itself is of little concern. What this often means is that a breach farther up the line results in an easily compromised storage system. For best resistance against attack, care must be taken at all levels.

People

By and large, the most vulnerable aspect of any computer system is its users. This includes not just the users who don't understand technology, but also the administrators who have grown lax. Passwords are written down; convincing requests for sensitive information are erroneously granted; inappropriate shortcuts are taken. One of the easiest and most common ways in which computers are breached is **social engineering**. Before undertaking a lot of complicated steps to steal your information, an attacker may try to simply ask you for it. People are trusting by nature, and often naively believe that anyone who asks has a legitimate reason to do so.

On the other side, malicious internal staff can be a serious threat. Disgruntled employees, especially those in the IT department, already have access to sensitive areas and information. If they have vengeance in mind, their goal may be disruption and destruction more than theft.

A starting point to security

Now that you have some idea of what you're up against, you can start thinking of how you want to approach the problems. The easiest thing to do is look over the preceding items and identify what your current configuration is weakest against. You'll also want to identify what your organization considers the most important points and data to protect. Once that's done, it's a good idea to perform some sort of an inventory in an attempt to discover sensitive points that may not have made the list for some reason or another. Sometimes, this can be done simply by asking questions such as "What would the impact be if someone saw that file?".

At all times, it's important to remember that there is no way a system can be truly secured without making it completely inaccessible to anyone. If even one person can get into the system, it's also possible for someone else. Computer security is not a one-time event; it is an ongoing process of re-evaluation.

It's also important to remember that computers are just machines. No matter how advanced the hardware and software is, the computer does not think. If an instruction makes it all the way to the CPU, it won't stop to ponder if the user or program that submitted it should be allowed to do so. It won't consider the moral implications of carrying out the instruction. It will simply do as it's told. Security is a human endeavor.

This book advocates both for taking specific steps to secure specific systems and for a **defense in depth** approach. The defense in depth style recognizes that not all attacks can be known or planned for in advance, so it attempts to mitigate them by using a layered strategy. If the firewall is penetrated, an internal network access control list may halt a break-in. If that doesn't work, intrusion prevention software may stop the attack. If that also fails, a simple password challenge may keep the intruder out.

Hyper-V terminology

Before we can properly discuss how to secure Hyper-V, we must reach an agreement on the words that we use. Terminology is a common point of confusion when it comes to Hyper-V and related technologies. This section will provide a definitive explanation for these terms, not only as they are used within this book, but also how they are generally used in official documentation and by experts.

Term	Definition
Hyper-V	The lone word **Hyper-V** represents the type 1 hypervisor technology developed and provided by Microsoft. This term does not refer to any particular product. It appears as an installable feature in Windows Server beginning with Version 2008, and in Professional and Enterprise desktop Windows operating system starting with version 8.
Hyper-V Server	**Hyper-V Server** is a standalone product available directly from Microsoft. It is a no-cost distribution of the hypervisor that is packaged in a heavily modified version of Windows Server.
Client Hyper-V	**Client Hyper-V** is the name given to Hyper-V as it appears in the desktop editions of Windows. The distinction is necessary as it has requirements and limitations that set it apart from Hyper-V as it exists in the server editions.
Host	The physical computer system that runs Hyper-V is called the **host**.
Guest	The term **guest** is often used interchangeably with "virtual machine." It is most commonly used to refer to the operating system inside the virtual machine.
Management operating system	As a type 1 hypervisor, Hyper-V is in direct control of the host's hardware and has no interface of its own. A **management operating system** is a special virtual machine that can interact with the hypervisor to control it and the hardware. In other hypervisors, this is known as the **parent partition**.

The commonly used term **Hyper-V Core** and variants have no official meaning. Core is a special mode for Windows Server that does not include a GUI. It is often used to refer to Hyper-V Server, as that product also has no GUI. Crossing Hyper-V Server with the core modifier should be avoided as it leads to confusion.

Acquiring Hyper-V

This book expects that you have some familiarity with Hyper-V and will therefore not provide an installation walkthrough. The purpose of this section is to provide a basic comparison of the delivery methods for Hyper-V so that you can make an informed decision in light of the security concerns.

Hyper-V Server

Hyper-V Server is freely available from Microsoft. It is a complete product and installs directly to the host computer. You can download it from the evaluation center on Technet at the following URL: `http://www.microsoft.com/en-us/evalcenter/evaluate-hyper-v-server-2012-r2`. Despite being listed alongside evaluation software, Hyper-V Server does not expire and does not require any product keys. Before installing, please read the system requirements, which are linked to the download page.

The reason why Hyper-V Server is often (erroneously) referred to as core is because it has no graphical interface of any kind. The only control options available on the console are the command-line and PowerShell. This is not the same thing as a Core installation of Windows as most of the Windows roles and features are not available.

There are a number of benefits and disadvantages to using Hyper-V in this fashion. The primary benefit in the realm of security is that there are fewer components in the base installation image and there are fewer potential weak points for an attacker to compromise.

Windows Server

Windows Server is Microsoft's general-purpose server software. Out of the box, it contains a great many server technologies and can fit into just about any conceivable server role. Among those offerings, you'll find Hyper-V.

Windows Server comes in two major editions with full Hyper-V support: Standard and Datacenter. The primary difference between these two is the licensing granted to guests that run Windows Server operating systems. Please consult a Microsoft licensing expert for more information. Technologically, the two editions are nearly identical. The lone difference is the presence of Automatic Virtual Machine Activation in the Datacenter edition, which allows it to activate Windows Server guests using its own license.

Windows Server can be installed in three separate modes: Core, Minimal Server Interface, and full GUI mode. Each of these modes affects the actions you must take to secure the system. Like Hyper-V Server, each has advantages and disadvantages.

Chapter 2, *Securing the Host*, will help you to decide between Hyper-V Server and one of the installation methods of Windows Server.

Client Hyper-V

Client Hyper-V is only available in Professional and higher desktop editions of Windows, but that's not all that makes it distinct from its cousin on the Server platforms. It requires a processor that can perform **Second Level Address Translation (SLAT)**. It also has a smaller feature set. Among the technologies not included are RemoteFX, Hyper-V Replica, and Live Migration. Client Hyper-V is also less inclined to consume all available host memory for the purpose of running guests.

While Client Hyper-V is not the focus of this book, many of the same concepts still apply. A very common use for Client Hyper-V is application development. Most software development firms consider their in-development programs to be highly valuable assets, so they should be as protected as any server-based asset.

Summary

This chapter introduced you to the "whys" of Hyper-V security and provided a brief introduction to the overall risks that almost all security systems face, and discussed generic responses. It also covered Hyper-V terminology and the available installation modes for the hypervisor.

In the next chapter, we'll dive right into Hyper-V security with a look at securing the physical host that runs the hypervisor.

2
Securing the Host

The Hyper-V host is easily the most critical component of your virtual environment. If it is compromised, all the systems in its scope of responsibility are placed at immediate risk. However, the Hyper-V host is, first and foremost, a computer system. Before diving into it as a computer that is running a hypervisor, it must be dealt with just like any other computer system. Of course, as it will run a hypervisor, particular considerations must be taken.

In this chapter, we'll cover the following topics:

- Understanding Hyper-V's architecture
- Choosing a management operating system
- Disabling unnecessary components
- Using the Windows Firewall
- Relying on domain security
- Leveraging Group Policy
- Using security software
- Configuring Windows Update
- Employing remote management tools
- Following general best practices

Understanding Hyper-V's architecture

Before you can address the security of your Hyper-V host, it's important to have a basic comprehension of Hyper-V architecture. Without this, it's difficult to understand how various security measures will affect the components of your deployment.

The most important thing to understand is that, for the most part, the hypervisor is independent of the management operating system. Hyper-V is a **type 1** hypervisor, which means that it is not an application or an operating system component. The hypervisor has direct control over the hardware it is installed on. It manages a number of **partitions**, which contain the virtual machines. One of these partitions, known as **parent partition**, is where the management operating system runs. The parent partition is the only partition that is allowed to communicate directly with the hypervisor. In Hyper-V, the parent partition provides the hardware drivers used by the hypervisor. To some extent, the parent partition does have direct access to the hardware, but Hyper-V is ultimately in charge of I/O. The distance between the management operating system and the hardware is most clearly seen on very large systems; even though Hyper-V can completely utilize physical hosts that have 320 logical processors and 4 TB of RAM, the management operating system will report no more than 64 logical processors and 1 TB of RAM—the same as any other virtual machine.

The following figure depicts a visualization of the relationships of the various components of a Hyper-V system:

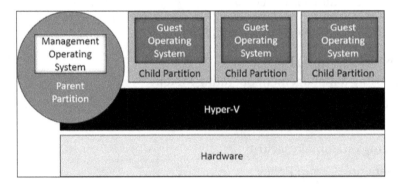

This chapter is dedicated to securing the management operating system. The important thing to understand from the preceding figure is that the actions you take at the host level will have the most impact on the management operating system's environment. Very little will be or can be changed that affects Hyper-V. The guests are isolated, so they will be almost completely unaffected.

Choosing a management operating system

In *Chapter 1, Introducing Hyper-V Security*, you were briefly introduced to the various delivery methods for Hyper-V in the *Acquiring Hyper-V* section. The first decision you must make before going into production is which of these methods you'll choose. This is not a clear choice, as each approach has its own strengths and weaknesses.

Hyper-V Server

In terms of security, the primary strength of Hyper-V Server is that it has a much smaller attack surface than even the smallest Windows Server deployment. This also has a side effect of having the fewest operating system components that could potentially compete with virtual machines for resources. Even though it's highly stripped-down compared to its full-featured counterpart, it does contain all the necessary options for running a Hyper-V environment, such as RemoteFX, the Remote Desktop Virtualization Host, and the ability to participate in a failover cluster.

The limitations that make Hyper-V Server more secure, however, also limit its appeal. There is no built-in GUI available on Hyper-V Server. While this increases the security of the system from a direct attack, it can also reduce the security of the host if the administrators responsible for it aren't sufficiently comfortable or knowledgeable to manage it properly. Frustration due to the lack of a familiar interface can lead to taking shortcuts that unnecessarily increase the risk to the host. For example, manipulating firewall rules from the command line can become overwhelming, so some administrators may take the single-line approach of disabling it entirely.

Another concern is that some of the features that are only found in Windows Server may be desirable to your Hyper-V environment. You should consider the fact that Microsoft does not support many roles alongside Hyper-V in the management operating system. One example of a Windows Server-only feature that is both supported and desirable in a Hyper-V environment is Data Deduplication. While Data Deduplication is currently only recommended when guests are running desktop operating systems (Virtual Desktop Infrastructure), it is supported for Hyper-V in 2012 R2 regardless of your usage. Another example is the Automatic Virtual Machine Activation feature of Windows Server Datacenter Edition.

If your Hyper-V Server stores its guests on a remote system, such as a SAN or an SMB 3 file server, that system can employ any Data Deduplication technology that it has available. The lack of availability of native Data Deduplication on Hyper-V Server only applies to the host's local storage.

Windows Server – full GUI installation

At the opposite end of the spectrum from Hyper-V Server is a complete installation of Windows Server with the Hyper-V role enabled. The primary reason most people choose this method is for the familiarity of the graphical interface. This does, of course, come at the cost of having the greatest attack surface of all possible deployment methods. The risk can be minimized by enabling no more roles or features than are necessary for the successful deployment and management of Hyper-V. Apart from the security benefits of this recommendation, Microsoft does not support the use of most of the other available components while Hyper-V is active.

Windows Server – Core installation

In current Windows versions, the default installation mode is Core. Like Hyper-V Server, this mode has no graphical interface of its own. However, most of the Windows Forms' components and application interfaces are still present, and the current versions of the .NET Framework can be installed, so applications that do not depend on the Microsoft Management Console or Internet Explorer will usually work normally.

While this is the smallest possible installation of Windows Server with the least attack surface, it is still larger than Hyper-V Server. This mode can be used to strike a compromise between the desire for higher security and the need for some supporting technologies that are only available in Windows Server, such as Data Deduplication. Do recall that, as previously mentioned, it is not supported to run many of the other Windows Server components on the host with Hyper-V.

Windows Server – Minimal Server Interface installation

Between the full and core installation options is **Minimal Server Interface**. One of the most common attack vectors on the Windows platform is Internet Explorer. By removing most of the features of Internet Explorer along with related components such as the Start screen and the desktop, some built-in graphical capabilities are retained while dramatically reducing the operating system's exposure. The **Microsoft Management Console** (**MMC**) application is available, which grants access to a number of tools such as Hyper-V Manager.

Switching between Windows Server modes

Before making your decision, keep in mind that you can convert Windows Server between any of its three modes with nothing more impacting than a system reboot. Hyper-V Server only provides the single GUI-less option.

You can use the **Features** page in the **Add Roles** and **Features** wizard or the **Remove Roles and Features** wizard to adjust these settings. Locate the **User Interfaces and Infrastructure** heading and expand it. Add or remove entries according to the desired mode using the following table as a guide:

System Modes	Graphical Management Tools and Infrastructure	Server Graphical Shell
Server Core Mode	No	No
Minimal Server Interface Mode	Yes	No
Full GUI Mode	Yes	Yes

You can also change these in PowerShell. Use the `Get-WindowsFeature` cmdlet to check the installation status of items. The cmdlets to be used to modify the changed status are `Add-WindowsFeature` and `Remove-WindowsFeature`. The feature names to use in PowerShell are as follows:

Display name	Feature name (used with PowerShell)
Graphical Management Tools and Infrastructure	`Server-Gui-Mgmt-Infra`
Server Graphical Shell	`Server-Gui-Shell`

An example of feature usage is:

```
Remove-WindowsFeature -Name Server-Gui-Mgmt-Infra, Server-Gui-Shell
```

> When the Graphical Management Tools and Infrastructure component is removed using the wizard, a warning box will notify you that all dependent MMC components, such as Hyper-V Manager, will also be removed. When it is removed using PowerShell, you are not warned.

For either method, be aware that if the operating system was initially installed in Core mode, you'll have to provide the source installation media to add the graphical files as they are not included by default.

Practical guidance to chose a deployment

There is no single correct answer in deciding between your available options. Before you start, it's a good idea to check whether the hardware that you'll be installing on is supported not only with Windows Server but also when the server is installed in Core mode. Anything that works in Core mode should also be supported with Hyper-V Server, but this can only be definitively confirmed by the hardware manufacturer.

The third-party software you intend to use on the system can also play a part. You should keep such software to minimum, but backup software or agents are largely unavoidable, and this may be true for anti-malware in some cases. Most software does work even on Core, as the Windows Forms Framework and API are available, but the Windows Presentation Framework is not.

Even if the hardware and software you intend to use does function on Server Core and Hyper-V Server, the manufacturer may not provide support for it. Ensure you check with the manufacturers of these tools before settling on a deployment method. A good place to start is the Windows Server Catalog, which is viewable at http://windowsservercatalog.com/. Items on this site are supported by both Microsoft and the manufacturer.

Two basic metrics to help you settle on a deployment method are the overall technical expertise level of your Windows Server administrators and your deployment's expected dependence on features. A basic conceptualization is shown in the following graph:

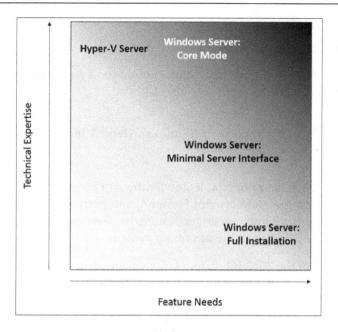

Of course, technical expertise levels will naturally improve through exposure, and your organization may be willing to make an investment in time and costs for training. The additional risks incurred through the larger attack surface of the more full-featured options are certainly present and must not be ignored, but they should not be treated as a major part of the decision for any institution except those already at a high risk. Files that are never accessed by the operating system do little for an attacker that manages to compromise them. In this light, you can reduce your risk by rigidly adhering to two rules. First, never enable additional roles and services. Second, fully remove old operating systems and replace them with newer versions instead of performing in-place upgrades

Disabling unnecessary components

A general rule in hardening any system is to turn off any system components that lack an identified, definite need. A good place to start narrowing this list to Hyper-V is with the list of roles that Microsoft doesn't support when Hyper-V is enabled. At this time, Microsoft has not published any official statement, but Hyper-V MVP Alessandro Cardoso has written an article on his blog that lists what roles are supported, viewable at `http://cloudtidings.com/2013/04/20/sharing-roles-with-hyper-v-on-the-same-physical-host/`. These items are:

- File and Storage Services
- Failover Clustering components

- Multipath I/O
- Remote Desktop Services

Although not specifically mentioned, management tools for all the preceding components as well as for Hyper-V are also allowed.

 If other roles or features are desired, install them in a virtual machine.

The simplest approach is to not enable any features or roles after installing the management operating system, except Hyper-V and entries from the preceding list. If you are repurposing an existing machine, the best tactic is to start with a completely fresh installation of the operating system.

Newly introduced in the 2012 R2 series of Server software is the ability to disable the outdated SMB 1.0/**CIFS (Common Internet File System)**. While not dramatically less secure than SMB 2.0, which cannot be disabled, this is an unnecessary feature for a typical Hyper-V host, as it's only used to communicate over SMB shares with Windows XP and Windows Server 2003. Turn it off on the **Features** page of the **Add Roles and Features** wizard in Server Manager. You can also disable it using PowerShell:

```
Remove-WindowsFeature -Name FS-SMB1
```

A reboot is typically required after making this change.

Third-party software is also a concern here. Tools such as backup and anti-malware are expected. Utilities such as ISO creation tools and applications such as web browsers are frivolous and should be left off entirely. Place programs that perform non-hypervisor functions and surf the Internet on a workstation or on another system that can be removed without impacting operations in the event that it is compromised.

Using the Windows Firewall

The Windows Firewall is a built-in component of both Hyper-V Server and Windows Firewall. While this tool is not as robust, secure, or powerful as high-end hardware firewalls, it is one of the better software firewalls available and is quite lightweight. It is possible to disable the functionality of the Windows Firewall, but completely disabling its service causes a number of problems. Since you're required to leave the service running, it's helpful to continue using it even when hardware firewalls are available as a low-cost part of a comprehensive defense-in-depth strategy.

Out of the box, the firewall automatically allows most remote management tools. For normal operations, it should require almost no maintenance. However, some steps can be taken to increase the protection it provides. For one thing, the default rules that enable inbound traffic are open to any source. This subject will be revisited in *Chapter 5, Securing the Network*, which is dedicated to the topic of networking.

Relying on domain security

Unfortunately, an all too common myth around Hyper-V security is that it is better to keep the Hyper-V host in workgroup mode. In reality, if an Active Directory domain is available, it is almost universally better to place all computer systems that are part of the local network into the domain, including the Hyper-V host. The lone exception is for systems that are so high-risk that it's almost expected that they'll be compromised. For these systems, the use of a **perimeter network** (also known as a **DMZ**) is a suitable solution. However, it is possible to use Hyper-V inside the local network while allowing all or some virtual machines to access only the perimeter. These options will be seen in *Chapter 5, Securing the Network*.

For systems that are within the local network, there are quite a few problems with using workgroup security when Active Directory services are available:

- Username and password combinations must be transmitted for remote connections; while usually encrypted, each transmission exposes these credentials to risks.

- Computer-to-computer authentication methods are typically one-way and are often not secure.

- Each computer system maintains its own database of user accounts without any central verification mechanism. In addition to being inherently less secure than Active Directory, records of these local accounts must be maintained and kept safe.

- Other security and system controls, such as Group Policy, must be established and updated individually on workgroup systems.

If a domain is available and the Hyper-V deployment will be hosting domain-joined guests, security is most easily handled if the host is a member of the domain as well. Instead of attempting to protect the domain by leaving the host unjoined, a better approach is to take the necessary steps to properly secure the host as a member.

If your deployment will be large-scale and you have the expertise available, another solution is to use a dedicated management domain. An extreme solution would be to use a completely separate forest. The benefits are that you have all the enhanced security that Active Directory can provide. The drawback is in the creation and management of security between domains and/or forests. The risk is that inter-domain and inter-forest trusts, if not managed and maintained properly, can actually make your deployment less secure than it would be if all systems were simply joined to the same domain. However, security in a multi-domain environment is still greater than that of a workgroup configuration.

If you choose to create a separate domain or forest, there is a solution that doesn't require the establishment of trusts, although remote management will be somewhat less convenient. Use a system on the management domain as a Remote Desktop host, configured with all the necessary tools to manage the systems. This configuration, sometimes known as a **jump host**, is shown in the following figure:

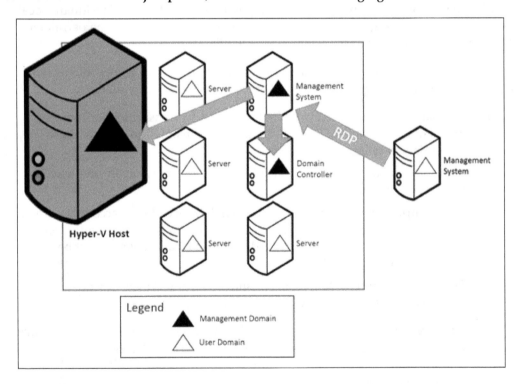

While the management system and the domain controller for the management domain are shown as guests of the Hyper-V host to be managed, this is not a necessity. You can use any mix of physical and virtual that makes sense in your deployment.

One thing that you must not do is configure the Hyper-V host as a domain controller. While allowed with Hyper-V in 2008 R2 and prior versions, it is specifically not supported beginning with 2012. The potential side effects of losing the local security database, which happens when a computer is converted to a domain controller, are unknown. Any security compromise of either the Active Directory components or Hyper-V would inevitably result in a breach to the other.

One of the benefits of using Active Directory is centralized Group Policy. This powerful tool gives you many capabilities in securing your hosts.

Leveraging Group Policy

Group Policy is a powerful tool that all Active Directory administrators should be familiar with. While it can be difficult to know which policies to set out of the thousands of available options, Microsoft has done a great deal of work for you with the **Microsoft Security Compliance Manager** (**SCM**). You can acquire this tool from `http://www.microsoft.com/scm`. The requirements and instructions for installation, as well as the download file, are given in the links provided on that page. Among the requirements is an installation of SQL Server. An Express installation is included in the package if you haven't got one available.

At the time of this writing, the current version of SCM is 3.0. Its package includes policies for Server and Hyper-V versions only through 2012. However, these policies will work just as well for the 2012 R2 versions. You can click on the **File** menu and then on **Check for Updates** to scan the Microsoft repository for any new baselines that may be available.

In the left pane of the main window, locate the entry named **Windows Server 2012** and expand it by clicking on the small triangle to its left. A number of sub entries will be displayed, as shown in the following screenshot:

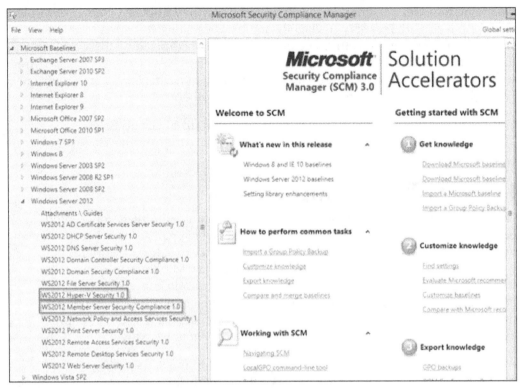

Sample configuration item

We are interested in two entries in particular. The first is titled **WS2012 Member Server Security Compliance 1.0**. If you click on it, the center pane will be updated to show the settings it contains. The settings are divided into various generic categories. Each line item represents a specific policy that will be modified. For these items, there are three columns that indicate the possible statuses of the policy. **Default** is the condition that the policy is in when Windows is initially installed and no changes are made. The **Microsoft** column shows Microsoft's recommended setting. The **Custom** column indicates what the policy will be set to if this baseline is exported and applied. Moving further to the right, the **Severity** column shows what level of importance Microsoft places on the setting.

If you click directly on any setting, it will expand to show the options for that item. Since this is a pre-generated baseline, items can't be modified. For more information on what's impacted by the setting you've selected, click on the downward-pointing arrow next to **Setting Details**. As shown in the following example screenshot, these often contain a great deal of extended information:

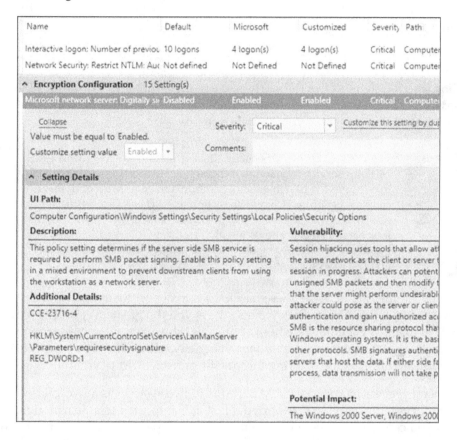

It should be safe to apply this generic member server baseline to all Hyper-V hosts because they should be running only a very limited set of roles, features, and applications. However, some third-party software may react poorly to these settings, and you may have other organizational requirements that preclude blanket application of the entire baseline. Pay special attention to the restrictions in the **User Rights Assignment** sub tree.

If you want to use only some and not all settings in a baseline, you have two options. First, you can apply the entire baseline, and then apply an overriding set of policies. This is not recommended as it can result in a difficult-to-manage Group Policy hierarchy. A better option is to create your own baseline by modifying those provided by Microsoft. If you want to make a change, you must first duplicate the existing baseline using the **Duplicate** link in the right pane, under the **Baseline** heading. You can then make any desired modifications to your newly created copy.

The second baseline that we're interested in is **WS2012 Hyper-V Security 1.0**. If you click on that, you'll see that it makes far fewer changes than the larger member server baseline, and it only modifies the startup status of a number of Windows services. These two baselines are completely compatible and you can use them together without setting any priorities or inheritance chains.

The WS2012 Hyper-V Security 1.0 baseline sets the **Microsoft iSCSI Initiator** service to manual. If this service is necessary, it is possible to override the baseline using additional SCM policies or to make changes in Group Policy. The section titled *Using Group Policy to control Hyper-V Administrators* in *Chapter 3, Securing Virtual Machines from the Hypervisor*, shows the preferred way to override these baselines. It may also be necessary to remove this setting entirely and use local settings.

The preferred method of using these baselines is to export them individually and import them into Group Policy. This allows you the greatest convenience of being able to apply each policy where applicable. However, it is possible to use the **Compare/Merge** option to join them into a single baseline. The only benefit to doing this is reduced effort in transferring these settings from SCM to your hosts.

The general process to apply an SCM baseline to live systems is a two-phase operation. First, the baseline is exported. Next, it is imported to a distribution tool. As you can see from the menu items in the right pane, there are a number of available options to export the baseline. We'll detail how to work with the GPO backup for Active Directory first, and then we'll show how to apply them to a standalone system.

Exporting SCM baselines

To export an SCM baseline to be used in Active Directory's Group Policy Management Console, the local Group Policy Editor, or the Microsoft Deployment Toolkit, perform the following steps:

1. In the left pane, click on the desired baseline to highlight it.
2. In the right pane, under **Export**, click on **GPO Backup folder**.

3. In the **Browse For Folder** dialog that appears, find a suitable location for the output files. Be aware that the output container will be a folder named GUID. So for ease of identification, it's recommended that you use the **Make New Folder** button to create a container with a friendly name. Directions in the later parts of this section will assume that you created a folder named Hyper-V Server Security.

The baseline has now been exported. Feel free to browse the folder structure to get an idea of what the tool did. The second phase is to import the policy into your distribution tool. If necessary, copy the data you created in step 3 to a location that is accessible to the system(s) that runs those tools.

Importing a policy into Group Policy Management Console

To import the policies for use in Active Directory, follow these steps:

1. Open the Group Policy Management Console. In the left pane, expand the forest that contains your Hyper-V hosts, then expand **Domains**, and finally, expand the domain that contains your Hyper-V hosts.

2. Right-click on **Group Policy Objects | New**. Give the policy a descriptive name that clearly indicates what it does. These directions will use SCM: Hyper-V Security.

3. Right-click on the newly created policy object and then click on **Import Settings....** Click on **Next** on the **Welcome** screen. As this is a new policy with nothing set, we can also click on **Next** on the **Backup GPO** screen without performing a backup.

4. On the Backup location screen, use the **Browse** button to navigate to the location you specified in step 3 of the export directions. Click on **Next**.

5. The **Source GPO** screen should show the GPO in the indicated folder. If it instead says that none were found, you may have selected one level too high or low in the folder structure in step 4. Click on **Back** to rectify this, or click on **Next** if the proper GPO is shown.

 The **View Settings** button will not work, as SCM does not create a gpreport.xml file.

6. The **Scanning Backup** screen should quickly complete its scan and warn you about security principals and UNC paths. Click on **Next**. On the **Migrating References** screen, leave the selection as **Copying them identically from the source**. The items found in the scan are well-known security principals and will not cause problems in your domain.

7. Click on **Next** and then on **Finish**. The import progress should take very little time. Click on **OK** once it's completed.

8. If you will be importing multiple baselines, this is the optimal point to repeat the preceding steps for the other(s).

9. Determine which **organizational unit** (**OU**) to apply the policy to. The member server security baseline can be applied to any 2012 or 2012 R2 member server while the Hyper-V security baseline should be restricted to hosts that run Hyper-V. Right-click on the desired GPO and click on **Link an Existing GPO…**.

10. In the **Select GPO** window, click on the new policy object. If you will be linking multiple GPOs, use *Ctrl* + click for additional objects. Click on **OK**.

The following screenshot that shows sample results of the preceding process was taken from a system in which all the Hyper-V hosts exist in the same top-level OU:

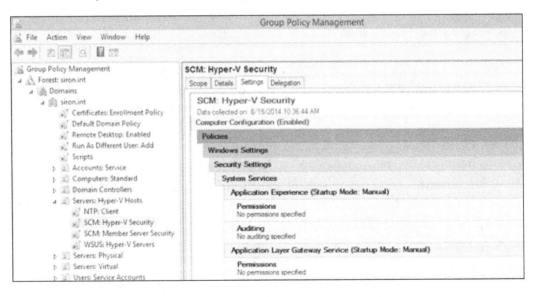

In a system with nested OUs, it is perfectly acceptable to only apply the member server baseline to a higher OU, and only apply the Hyper-V baseline to a sub-OU that contains the Hyper-V systems. Unless inheritance is blocked, the sub-OU will receive the settings from its parent and apply them along with those that are directly linked. Because these policies modify startup settings, the affected hosts should also be rebooted when possible.

Once all the policies have been set in Group Policy, you can simply wait for the policies to apply naturally. By default, this will occur within 90 minutes. You can force the application of the policy on individual hosts by running gpupdate /force from their respective command lines.

Applying SCM baselines to Local Group Policy

If the Hyper-V host is not domain-joined, or if you are preparing a master system for the **Sysprep** tool, SCM includes the LocalGPO tool. In the **Start** menu or **Start** screen for the system where you installed SCM, you'll find an entry for LocalGPO. When you open it, you'll be taken to a Windows Explorer folder that contains LocalGPO. msi. Copy this installer to the target system where you want to apply the exported baselines, and run the installation.

When installed, the tool creates a Local GPO folder under the root's Program Files (x86) folder. Inside this folder is a script file named LocalGPO.wsf. This is the tool that you'll use to work with the exported baselines. As an example, if the WS2012 Hyper-V Security 1.0 baseline was exported to a folder named C:\Users\ Administrator\Documents\Hyper-V Server Security, the command line will be similar to the following (the GUID is randomly generated):

```
LocalGPO.wsf /Path:"C:\Users\administrator\Documents\Hyper-V Server
Security\{2b973f2e-b4b3-485f-a230-6f762e78cec3}"
```

 By placing a space after /Path:, you can use the *Tab* key while typing the path for auto-complete assistance with long folder names. Remember to delete the space before pressing *Enter* or the script will throw an error.

You will be reminded to reboot, as there are startup policies being changed.

Enabling LocalGPO in Windows and Hyper-V Server 2012 R2

The LocalGPO script is coded to only run on particular versions of Windows, and at this time, it does not recognize the 2012 R2 server products. You'll need to manually edit the script to remove this check; use the following steps to do this:

1. Use Notepad or some other text editor to open the script. From Windows Explorer, you can right-click on `LocalGPO.wsf` and click on `Edit`. On Hyper-V Server or Windows Server in Core mode, navigate to the folder of the `LocalGPO` folder and type `notepad LocalGPO.wsf`.

2. Press *Ctrl + F* to open the search box. Type `Call ChkOSVersion` in the box and click on **OK**.

3. Place a semicolon on the located line anywhere to the left of the text. This should look like what is shown in the following screenshot:

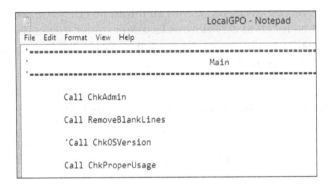

4. Save the file (*Ctrl + S*) and close Notepad.

Once you complete these steps, you will now be able to run the script on 2012 R2.

Using security software

The recommendations for the use of additional security software on a Hyper-V host are not unanimous among experts. You will need to weigh the pros and cons against your organization's particular situation.

These are some of the major concerns around using security software:

- Hyper-V hosts are responsible for providing resources to a number of guest machines. Any software in the management operating system, no matter how beneficial, will compete for these resources.

- Virtual machines are highly dependent upon the filesystem of the management operating system, and the intervention of an anti-malware application could cause them to become completely lost.

- An initially successful deployment of anti-malware software could later be broken by an update to its detection algorithms or engine.

- Hyper-V can be effectively isolated from other systems and still expose its virtual machines, effectively placing the greatest need for security on upstream exposure points.

Some of the considerations that support usage of such software are:

- Your organization may be subject to regulatory or other legal requirements to use some form of security software without exception

- Hyper-V is not the only software that is at risk from misconfigured or over-eager anti-malware, and like most other systems, there are steps that can be taken to ensure it successfully cooperates

- A thorough defense-in-depth approach would not rely solely on upstream systems for security

Microsoft has not published an official exclusions list for anti-malware application for recent versions of Hyper-V Server. A community-maintained list does exist in the TechNet wiki, which can be viewed at `http://social.technet.microsoft.com/wiki/contents/articles/2179.hyper-v-anti-virus-exclusions-for-hyper-v-hosts.aspx`. Additionally, Hyper-V can be joined into a Microsoft Failover Cluster configuration. Microsoft publishes an official guideline for anti-malware usage on cluster nodes, available at `http://support.microsoft.com/kb/250355`.

While the wiki article does indicate that the configuration folders for virtual machines should be excluded, it helps to take additional steps to ensure that their XML files are explicitly excluded. This could be achieved using a global exemption for XML files or by targeting the folder structure(s) where virtual machines reside.

The wiki article only covers file exclusions, which applies to the scanning of file contents. Most modern anti-malware packages also watch the in-memory activity of executables for suspicious behavior, and this can interfere with Hyper-V's operations. Consult with your anti-malware manufacturer for the proper steps to exclude VMMS.EXE and VMWP.EXE from such monitoring.

Your anti-malware software vendor may also provide specific information on configuring their product for use on a Hyper-V host. If possible, consult with their support or engineering teams to learn whether they have any specific history and advice for this scenario.

Software that runs constantly on the local system isn't the only type of security software available. Later in this chapter, we'll look at Microsoft Baseline Security Analyzer, which scans one or more systems for known vulnerabilities and misconfigurations. There are a number of third-party tools that perform similar functions against substantially larger templates. As they usually don't use components directly on your hosts, the greatest risk these tools usually present is an extra load on system resources while scans are run. In a high-security organization, this cost is likely to be outweighed by the benefits.

Microsoft also publishes the **Enhanced Mitigation Experience Toolkit (EMET)** at `http://www.microsoft.com/emet`. This is a complicated tool that aggregates several advanced threat mitigation techniques. Due to the size and complexity of EMET, it won't be elaborately discussed in this book. The documentation that accompanies the download and the resources linked from the launch page provides plenty of guidance.

While EMET does provide definite protections, its primary purpose is to block application-level attacks, especially those that target Internet Explorer. As you shouldn't be running such applications on a Hyper-V host anyway, EMET may not be an appropriate solution. However, as part of a defense-in-depth strategy, it may have its merits. EMET will run on a Hyper-V host with the maximum protection settings without impeding hypervisor or guest operations. You will need to weigh the potential security benefits against the potential for performance impacts on your selected hardware.

Configuring Windows Update

Microsoft provides patches to the currently supported operating systems and other products on a regular basis. Most of these are made available on the second Tuesday of each month, or what has come to be known as "Patch Tuesday". This is the typical release cycle for most security-related patches as well, although truly critical updates can be made available at any time. The standard delivery method for these patches is Windows Update. Access to this repository can be entirely automated, if desired.

Unfortunately, Microsoft's track record of releasing quality updates is somewhat spotty. Some have rendered systems to be completely unusable. For a Hyper-V host, this could have catastrophic effects. On the other hand, not applying security updates places the system at a high risk of compromise. Many vulnerabilities already have known exploits before they are ever patched, but the publication of a patch often leads to a rash of malware intended to exploit the very vulnerability that it addresses. As a result, you must weigh the overall risks to your system. There are a number of approaches you can take to mitigate your exposure, each with its own pros and cons.

Manual patching

Of all the available options, this is the most time-consuming for system administrators. You can use the in-system Windows Update tool to connect to the repository. It displays a list of all the available patches and their **knowledge base (KB)** numbers. By searching the Internet for these KB numbers, you can determine whether others are reporting problems. Once you've determined that a patch is safe, you can manually download and apply it.

A variant of this is to allow Windows to download the patches but wait for approval to install them. This saves some time, but still requires quite a bit of effort on your part.

Another variant is to use **Windows Server Update Services (WSUS)** in the manual approval mode. This considerably reduces your overall load, as you can approve individual patches for entire groups of systems or even your entire domain, all at once.

Manual patching is not recommended as fatigue and forgetfulness are more likely to result in a compromised system than the occasional bad patch.

Fully automated patching

It is possible to simply set all systems to automatically apply all available patches. Even the worst patches typically don't negatively impact all systems, and most of the undesirable effects aren't so crippling that they can't be corrected. While this is a somewhat risky approach, it errs on the side of greater security.

Staggered patching

If you have multiple systems available, you can use the scheduling capabilities of Group Policy to set some systems to patch before others. Unfortunately, this will need to be set, maintained, and documented per-system, but it's automatic after that.

To set this schedule, open Group Policy Editor on a GUI system (run `gpedit.msc`). Navigate to **Local Computer Policy** | **Administrative Templates** | **Windows Components** | **Windows Update**. Set the options under **Configure Automatic Updates** as desired. Setting the date to Monday or very early on Tuesday morning (depending on your time zone) will give you nearly a full week after patches are published before they are applied. Unfortunately, this doesn't protect well against patches released on days apart from "Patch Tuesday", but due to the high criticality of such updates, the risk may be worth it.

By setting some systems earlier than others, you can monitor them for negative effects before your other systems are placed at risk while still enjoying fully automated patch deployment.

Guinea pig systems

An option that works best when used in conjunction with WSUS is the use of designated "guinea pigs" or test systems. These can be set to use fully automated patching through the usage of automatic approvals. All other systems can be set for manual approvals. Once it's determined that a patch round is clean, you can manually approve the patches for all the other systems or initiate the application of an automatic approval rule against their WSUS containers.

Employing remote management tools

One way to reduce your hosts' exposure to risks is to simply stay off them. The more the local consoles are used, the more likely is the administrator to become complacent and start using poor practices such as surfing the Internet from a mission-critical host. Risks such as this also serve as another reason to use Hyper-V Server or Windows Server in Core mode.

When the host is in the same domain as the remote management system, most remote tools work without modification. The firewall defaults to allowing most of the MMC-based management tools. The only restriction is that the user account must have the proper rights on the host. If the machines are in different domains, more work must be done. As these tools cross the network, and security is checked at that point, we'll revisit this subject and provide direction in *Chapter 5, Securing the Network*.

The free tools from Microsoft require that the remote system be at the same operating system level as the target for complete management. For example, Windows 7 can manage a 2008 R2 host and Windows 8.1 can manage a 2012 R2 host. Starting with Windows 8 / Windows / Hyper-V Server 2012, a remote system can manage the features of a higher system that it is aware of, and a newer system can remotely manage some earlier systems. These tools are already built in the Windows Server; they just need to be enabled under **Remote Server Administration Tools** on the **Features** page of the **Add Roles and Features** wizard. For desktop operating systems, refer to Microsoft's download page at http://www.microsoft.com/download. Search for the version of **Remote Server Administration Tools** that matches with your desktop operating system version. Once installed, they'll appear in the **Turn Windows features on or off** applet in the Control Panel.

Following general best practices

As mentioned earlier in this chapter, the security steps you are taking here apply primarily to the management operating system. While it does run Hyper-V, it is still a computer system. Therefore, most of the steps that would be taken on a standard Windows Server system apply just as well to a Hyper-V host.

Microsoft baseline security analyzer

As with Group Policy, there are a dizzying array of options, and it's difficult to keep track of them all. In terms of security, Microsoft has provided a tool to help with this as well: **Microsoft Baseline Security Analyzer (MBSA)**. The current version of this tool is available from Microsoft at `http://www.microsoft.com/mbsa`.

The installation procedure for MBSA is extremely straightforward and won't be outlined here. There are no special prerequisites. You can run the tool from a system other than the one to be scanned, although you'll likely get incomplete results due to firewall issues. You must start MBSA with a user account that has administrative privileges on the target system(s), or many tests will fail. The following screenshot shows the results of a scan against a test system:

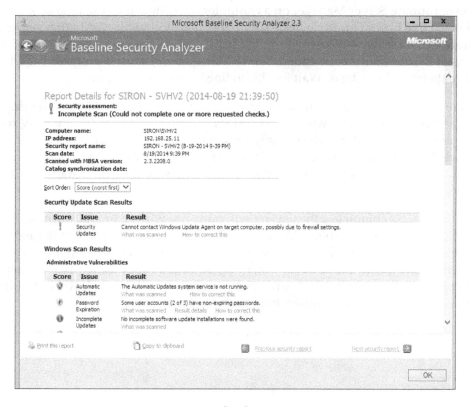

For each finding, there is a hyperlink for **What was scanned**. Items that indicate a problem also have one labeled **How to correct this**. These index into a general help file that details the scanning process and remedies for common issues.

Once a scan has been run, it will be saved locally. These can be seen later from the main MBSA screen using the hyperlink on the left side labeled **View security reports**. Reports can be printed and placed on the clipboard for use in another application. MBSA scans should be performed periodically to catch any configuration changes that might have exposed the system.

Hyper-V Best Practices Analyzer

New beginning with the 2012 server series is a built-in **Best Practices Analyzer (BPA)** just for Hyper-V (as well as a number of other analyzers). This tool will scan a Hyper-V host, looking for common misconfigurations, and provide a report. Security is not the primary focus of this tool, but it will uncover obvious problems. It can be used from Server Manager or from within PowerShell.

Running the Hyper-V BPA from Server Manager

If you're running Server Manager on a computer other than the system to be scanned, or if you'd like to scan multiple hosts simultaneously, follow the **Add other servers to manage** tool from the **Welcome** tile on the home page of Server Manager. Once all the necessary systems have been added, Server Manager will show a progress bar while it loads data from those hosts. Wait for this to finish before proceeding.

Click on the **Hyper-V** tab on the left-hand side of Server Manager. This will bring you to a **Servers** page that lists all the connected systems that run the Hyper-V role. Scroll down to the **Best Practices Analyzer** section. Under the **Tasks** menu at the far right, click on **Start BPA scan**. This will pop up a box that shows the available hosts to scan. Use the checkboxes to select the desired targets and click on **Start Scan** to begin scanning.

Once the process completes, the list box will populate with error and warning conditions. As with any other BPA in Server Manager, you can use the filter tools to change what is shown. The complete results cannot be saved here, but you can right-click on any line item and click on **Copy Results Properties** to place the details of that item on the system's clipboard. The results are saved in an XML file, but it's best to use the PowerShell cmdlets to output them.

Running the Hyper-V BPA from PowerShell

PowerShell exposes far more capabilities of the BPA than Server Manager does, but it is more difficult to use.

To initiate a scan (the referenced BPAResults folder must already exist), use the following code:

```
Invoke-BPAModel -ComputerName svhv1, svhv2 -ModelId Microsoft/Windows/
Hyper-V -RepositoryPath C:\BPAResults
```

To retrieve the results of a scan, use the following code:

```
Get-BPAResult -ModelId Microsoft/Windows/Hyper-V -RepositoryPath C:\
BPAResults
```

If you have saved multiple reports to the same location, you can use the -All parameter to see everything. Otherwise, only the latest report is retrieved.

To make the XML files more user friendly, you can pipe them to the various formatting tools built in PowerShell or to third-party formatting cmdlets. Some examples are as follows:

```
Get-BPAResult -ModelId Microsoft/Windows/Hyper-V -RepositoryPath C:\
BPAResults | Out-GridView
```

```
Get-BPAResult -ModelId Microsoft/Windows/Hyper-V -RepositoryPath
C:\BPAResults | Convert-ToCsv | Out-File -PSPath C:\BPAResults\
AllHostsHyperVBPA.csv
```

```
Get-BPAResult -ModelId Microsoft/Windows/Hyper-V -RepositoryPath
C:\BPAResults | Convert-ToHtml | Out-File -PSPath C:\BPAResults\
AllHostsHyperVBPA.html
```

Other practices

While certainly not an exhaustive list, the following is a sample list of generic best practices that apply to Hyper-V hosts:

- Perform regular scans for known problems. Use tools such as SCM and BPA. BPA is the easiest as PowerShell can be used to automate scans.

- Carefully select individuals with administrative access to the hosts. Periodically review the list and remove any entries that should no longer have access.

- Develop and codify your approach to local accounts. When a domain is available, it is best to simply use domain accounts and place them into local security groups. However, there are other considerations:

  ○ Consider renaming the local administrator account. This is a "security by obscurity" technique that doesn't improve security much, but it is simple and harmless, and adds a tiny amount to a defense-in-depth paradigm.

  ○ Avoid disabling the local administrator account. This can have unforeseen consequences without meaningfully improving security.

  ○ Rename and disable the guest account.

  ○ Decide whether or not to use a single password for all (or groups) of hosts' administrator accounts or to use a unique password for each. There is no universal consensus. If all systems use the same password, then a breach of one could lead to a breach of all. However, unique passwords require a great deal of maintenance that usually involves a centralized data store of some kind. If that repository is breached, all hosts are breached. Whatever path you choose, ensure it is set as an organization policy and all administrators adhere to it.

  ○ Consider using Group Policy to disable cached credentials. This can have negative consequences if the domain is ever unavailable and the local administrator account is also not usable, but it prevents anyone's credentials from being hijacked by an attacker that compromises the cache. Remember that Hyper-V and its guests will continue to run even if the host is unable to log in to the domain.

  ○ Be wary of domain-pushed policies that affect items in **Computer Configuration | Windows Settings | Security Settings | Local Policies | User Rights Assignment**, particularly **Create symbolic links**. By default, this policy grants rights to a local Virtual Machines account, which is not visible or controllable from the domain. Making changes to the other groups via a domain-enforced policy can have other unintended side effects. If you want to use Group Policy to manage local groups and users, use the tools on the domain GPO under **Computer Configuration | Preferences | Control Panel Settings | Local Users and Groups** instead, as these allow you to modify custom entries without damaging existing ones.

- Document everything. This should include the initial configuration and every configuration change made to the host.

- Treat security configuration as an ongoing event, not a one-time process. Use your calendar to schedule recurring security audits and documentation verification.

- Only use a host for its designated purpose. It should not be your primary workstation, its web browser should remain closed, and it should not even temporarily run unrelated software.

- Realize that perfect security is impossible. Any system that be reached by a legitimate user can be compromised by a determined and skilled attacker, and sometimes just a lucky one. Threat response is as important as threat preparation and prevention.

- Remember that best practices lists are guidelines, not fixed, unbreakable rules. The final arbiter of whether or not a practice is "best" is how well it suits the needs of your organization.

- Research! Stay on top of Microsoft security bulletins by regularly accessing their security site at `http://msdn.microsoft.com/en-us/bb291012.aspx`. Find and follow security experts on Twitter. Attend training classes where applicable. Seek out new security resources.

Summary

This chapter introduced you to a number of concepts related to securing a Hyper-V host. First, we talked about the scope of security in Hyper-V and explained that the management operating system is secured much like any other computer. Next, we discussed the available choices of the management operating system and how they impact security. We followed that up with a discussion on disabling components that aren't necessary for running Hyper-V. Then, we briefly visited the subject of the Windows Firewall. Next, we examined the benefits of Active Directory membership for Hyper-V hosts, which led directly into a discussion of Group Policy and how it can be easily leveraged for Hyper-V hosts. We talked about using third-party security software, such as anti-malware and intrusion-detection programs. We also discussed how to use Windows Update to keep Microsoft software up to date. Afterwards, we touched on using remote tools instead of connecting directly to the host console. We wrapped up the chapter with a discussion on general best practices.

Before we end the discussion of securing the host, it should be stated that this chapter is intended as the starting point, not the final word. There are always more things to consider and discover. There are always new attack vectors being uncovered. There are always other ways your systems could be placed in danger.

In the next chapter, we'll look at ways to configure Hyper-V to protect its guests.

3
Securing Virtual Machines from the Hypervisor

As the container for the virtual machines, the hypervisor is the natural starting point when you begin the task of securing guests. Much like the previous chapter, many of the techniques used are along the lines of those you'd use in other contexts. In this case, instead of following the common practices to secure hosts, you'll be working on securing an application. This application is Hyper-V.

In this chapter, we'll be discussing the following:

- Using the Hyper-V Administrators group
- Leveraging PowerShell Remoting
- Using custom PowerShell Remoting endpoints

Using the Hyper-V Administrators group

Beginning with the 2012 series of servers, Hyper-V Server or any Windows Server with the Hyper-V role enabled will have an automatically created local security group named "Hyper-V Administrators." The purpose of this account is to allow you to assign the capability to manage Hyper-V and its virtual machines without opening the floodgates all the way to allow complete control over the host.

Downloading the example code

You can download the example code files for all Packt books you have purchased from your account at http://www.packtpub.com. If you purchased this book elsewhere, you can visit http://www.packtpub.com/support and register to have the files e-mailed directly to you.

Using Group Policy to control Hyper-V Administrators

If you followed the guidance from the previous chapter, you may have assigned the "WS2012 Member Server Security Compliance 1.0" baseline to your Hyper-V hosts. If you made no changes to that, it prevents anyone except members of the built-in Administrators group from logging in directly to the console or through Remote Desktop connections—even the built-in Remote Desktop Users group is disallowed. A quick workaround would be to place members of the Hyper-V Administrators group into the local Administrators group, but doing this defeats the purpose of using that group.

It is not possible to nest the local Hyper-V Administrators group inside other built-in groups such as Administrators and Remote Desktop Users.

It is not necessary to grant the members of Hyper-V Administrators the right to log in locally or through Remote Desktop. The standard management tools, **Hyper-V Manager** and **Failover Cluster Manager**, can be run from remote systems without the need to modify anything in the default security settings or SCM's baselines.

If you wish to override the behavior of the baseline, you can either create another Group Policy Object that will be applied after the baseline GPO or modify the existing one. If you choose to create another GPO, it needs to be set on a lower organizational unit than the baseline or be higher in the link order list (lower **Link Order** number) when applied to the same GPO. The following screenshot of the Group Policy Management Console shows how this precedence can be properly set with Link Order:

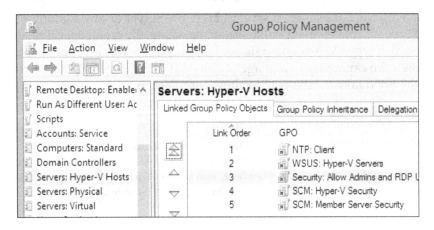

To change the policy itself, open the Group Policy Management Editor for the new GPO. Navigate to **Computer Configuration | Policies | Windows Settings | Security Settings | Local Policies | User Rights Assignment**. The name of the local logon policy is **Allow log on locally** while the Remote Desktop policy is **Allow log on through Remote Desktop Services**. Our example environment does not modify the local policy as it's generally best to restrict console access to administrators. An example configuration of the Remote Desktop policy is shown as follows:

Be aware that the entries under the User Rights Assignment branch are exclusive. Only the highest priority policy will apply, and all others will be ignored. Any group or account not specifically included in the list will be excluded. As an example, if the Administrators group was removed from the previous example, administrators would be prevented from logging in through Remote Desktop. Use these security settings with extreme caution.

It is possible to simply modify the baseline policy assigned from the Security Compliance Manager so that the **Allow log on through Remote Desktop Services** setting is not defined. However, such an action must be documented and carefully maintained so that future direct updates from later revisions to the baseline do not break established settings. While more effort is required initially, layered policies result in a more resilient system.

While it's tempting and possible to just add the Hyper-V Administrators group to the same policy as Administrators and Remote Desktop Users, doing this will have no effect. Setting this policy does not override the fact that the Hyper-V Administrators group cannot be nested inside Remote Desktop Users, so there is no way to specifically allocate this permission directly to that group.

Once all the preceding permissions are set, the next step is to place the desired user accounts into the Hyper-V Administrators group, and if desired, into the Remote Desktop Users group on each host. This can be accomplished through the Local Users and Group tool (`lusrmgr.msc`) directly on each GUI-based host or by using `mmc.exe` to attach this or the larger Computer Management snap-in to the remote computer. However, a better way is to leverage Group Policy.

Follow these steps from within Group Policy Management Console:

1. Under the desired domain, right-click on **Group Policy Objects** and click on **New**. Name the policy as something that indicates its purpose. Our sample environment uses **Security: Set Hyper-V Administrators**. Now, click on **OK**.

2. Right-click on the newly created Group Policy object and click on **Edit...**.

3. Expand **Computer Configuration**, then expand **Preferences**, and finally expand **Control Panel Settings**.

4. Right-click on **Local Users and Groups** and then go to **New | Local Group**.

5. Leave **Action** set to **Update**. In the **Group Name** field, type `Hyper-V Administrators`. Alternatively, if you are performing these steps from a system with the Hyper-V role enabled, you can use the **...** button next to **Group Name** to browse the local system for this group.

6. Below the empty **Members** listbox, click on **Add...**.

7. In the **Local Group Member** dialog that appears, type or browse for the domain user(s) or domain group(s) to be added to this group. Leave **Action** set to **Add to this group**. Click on **OK**.

8. Verify that the **Members** listbox is now populated with the items you added from step 7. Click on **OK**.

9. Back in the **Group Policy Management Editor** screen, verify that the preference policy appears in the **Local Users and Groups** list. Close **Group Policy Management Editor**.

10. Back in the main **Group Policy Management** window, locate the Organizational Unit that the policy should be applied to. Right-click on it and select **Link an Existing GPO...**. Select the GPO named in step 1 and click on **OK**.

11. Wait for the policy to update automatically or force an update on one of the affected systems with `gpupdate /force`. Check the local groups to verify that the changes are applied as expected, as shown in the following screenshot:

If you wish for these users to also be able to log in using Remote Desktop, repeat these steps to add them into that local group. Unlike Hyper-V Administrators, you will be able to select the pre-existing Remote Desktop Users group from the drop-down box in step 5.

There are a number of benefits to using this approach as opposed to manually maintaining accounts on local systems:

- With Active Directory serving as a central repository for local group membership, setting, documenting, and maintaining local group membership is greatly simplified
- When the need arises, Group Policy can be used to quickly rescind membership across multiple machines

> For emergency situations such as termination of an employee that has shown to be a security risk and might still be connected to systems, start by disabling the user's **Active Directory** account. This action takes effect immediately without waiting for a policy refresh.

- Group Policy can be used to restrict group membership so that even local administrators cannot exert control

We didn't cover all the options available using Group Policy preferences. Spend some time exploring the dialog boxes and options. While the actions we showed will simply add user accounts to any entries that are already present, you can also use the options here to remove membership from any users or groups except those that you specify. You can use additional entries to remove specific accounts for which you want to revoke permissions.

> Create one or more security groups at the domain level for the purpose of managing Hyper-V. Add individual user accounts to these groups. Place these groups, not individual accounts, into the local computer groups. This dramatically reduces the overall administrative effort.

Powers of Hyper-V Administrators

The powers of Hyper-V Administrators are pretty simple to understand. Anything accessible in Hyper-V Manager can be controlled by a member of this group. Virtual machines' power states (off, on, and saved) can be changed, and the Hyper-V-related host settings can be modified. With some caveats, which will be discussed in the upcoming section on SMB 3 storage, virtual machines can be created and destroyed. However, if a guest is clustered, not all of its settings are accessible in Hyper-V Manager. Fortunately, the necessary PowerShell cmdlets do the work. Out-of-the box, this will require you to perform the preceding steps to enable members of Hyper-V Administrators to access the system through Remote Desktop, as PowerShell Remoting is only available to members of the local Administrators group. As you'll see in the next section, this isn't a problem without a solution.

It may be more important to discuss what Hyper-V Administrators cannot do, as not all the restrictions will be obvious to everyone. Members of this group have no administrative access on the host itself. They cannot modify drivers, create or modify network adapter teams, or even restart the computer. They have the same access that most standard users have on a server computer, which is highly restricted. Members are able to perform **Shared Nothing Live Migrations** of non-clustered virtual machines, although they must be in the Hyper-V Administrators group (or Administrators) on both the source and destination host. What may come as a surprise is that members of Hyper-V Administrators cannot perform **Live Migration** across cluster nodes. The necessary interfaces and cmdlets are simply inaccessible.

Leveraging PowerShell Remoting

The complete scope of PowerShell Remoting is far beyond the limits of this book. What you'll see here is enough to get you started with Hyper-V, and depending on your skill with PowerShell, this may be all that you need. There are a vast number of resources available online. You are encouraged to research this topic on your own for more information. Good starting places are TechNet (`http://technet. microsoft.com`) and `http://PowerShell.org`. One subject that we won't be spending time on is **implicit remoting**, in which you use the `-ComputerName` parameter built in many PowerShell cmdlets.

PowerShell Remoting is a feature of PowerShell that allows you to use PowerShell on one computer to issue commands to one or more target computers just as though you were sitting directly at those consoles.

Configuring PowerShell Remoting and its basic usage

Before you can use PowerShell Remoting at all, you first need to enable your hosts. At an elevated PowerShell prompt, type the following:

```
Enable-PSRemoting -Force
```

You may receive an indication that one or more of the settings have already been configured. This needs to be done on both the system(s) to be controlled and on the system(s) that you'll use as a control computer. If they are all in the same domain, then no further configuration is necessary unless you have internal firewalls. PowerShell Remoting works over the WinRM port, which is TCP/5985. This port is open by default in the Windows Firewall.

Once the systems are prepared, you can initiate an interactive remote PowerShell session using the following syntax:

```
Enter-PSSession -ComputerName svhv1
```

The preceding cmdlet will use the same credentials with which you are logged on to the local computer. If that account isn't an Administrator on the target, use the following cmdlet instead:

```
Enter-PSSession -ComputerName svhv1 -Credential (Get-Credential)
```

On pressing *Enter*, you will be prompted for the credentials that you wish to use. Domain credentials should be entered in the format DOMAIN\USERNAME.

As previously mentioned, the created session is interactive. The PowerShell prompt will be modified to show the target computer's name to make you aware that you are working remotely. Once connected, you can issue any PowerShell cmdlets that are available on the target system, even if they're not present on the source system. You can also start simple processes, although you will not be able to use anything that contains its own GUI or shell.

Once you have finished working remotely, you can close the window or issue the Exit-PSSession cmdlet. This cmdlet has a convenient exit alias.

To perform operations simultaneously on many computers, use Invoke-Command:

```
Invoke-Command -ComputerName svhv1, svhv2 -ScriptBlock { Get-VM | Start-VM }
```

While not shown here, Invoke-Command can also utilize the -Credential parameter. The script block can be very complicated. To make it easier, you can store entire blocks inside a variable that you pass to the Invoke-Command cmdlet. An example is shown towards the end of this section.

Unlike Enter-PSSession, Invoke-Command will automatically close all the remote sessions when it is initiated, as shown earlier.

PowerShell Remoting allows you to create sessions in advance with New-PSSession. Invoke-Command can then connect to those sessions with the -Session parameter. This is especially useful if you need to send the same commands to multiple hosts using different credentials. Unlike the earlier usage, Invoke-Command does not automatically close sessions when -Session is used.

PowerShell remote sessions validate not only the user account but also the target computer's account. Within the same domain, Kerberos will handle this automatically. For targets that are in a workgroup, such as computers in a perimeter network or for systems in another domain, more work needs to be done to enable the remote session.

All of the cmdlets shown in this section have a number of other options, most of which won't be discussed here. You can start your exploration with the built-in help files, which can be viewed as follows:

```
Get-Help Enter-PSSession -Full
```

Another issue you might encounter is saving credentials so that you don't need to re-enter them each time you want to start a remote session. The PowerShell community has provided a number of approaches to store credential sets in a somewhat secure fashion. None of them are included here as none of those methods are official, and any technique that saves credentials for automated retrieval is inherently insecure. Before using any of them, ensure that you are aware of the risks, and that any restrictions (legal or self-imposed) that your organization is required to be in compliance with are not violated by their usage.

Workgroup and inter-domain PowerShell Remoting

Because machine-level authentication is required for PowerShell Remoting, enabling this feature between computers that aren't on the same domain requires a number of additional steps as Kerberos isn't available. There are two options. We'll explore the most secure option first.

Certificate-based PowerShell Remoting

In its simplest form, certificate-based PowerShell Remoting requires the target system to present a certificate to the connecting system that was issued by a certificate authority trusted by the connecting system. Once this prerequisite has been met, initiating a remote session is as simple as this:

```
Enter-PSSession -ComputerName svhv1 -UseSSL -Credential (Get-Credential)
```

The challenge is in moving the certificates around as necessary. If your organization is already utilizing **public key infrastructure** (**PKI**), the barrier to entry is notably lower. If you aren't using PKI and don't have the necessary expertise, it is also possible to use certificates issued by a public authority.

Configuring the Host SSL certificate

If the target computer (in our usage, a Hyper-V host) is a member of the domain, and PKI is configured for auto-enroll, it may already have a certificate. For other uses, a certificate can be requested using the MMC snap-in. We perform the following steps to configure the Host SSL certificate:

1. Log in to any Windows system with a GUI. From the **Run** or **Start** menu, type mmc.exe and press *Enter* (if your current user account doesn't have administrative privileges on the target machine, use **Run As Administrator** or **Run As a Different User** as necessary).

 If you cannot start MMC using the credentials of the target system, such as for a Hyper-V Server in a perimeter network, you can choose to proceed by selecting **Local Computer** on step 5, following the custom path in step 7, and entering in the name(s) of the system to issue the certificate for in steps 14 and 15. It is mandatory that you make the private key exportable in step 17. This will allow you to use your current computer to create a certificate on behalf of the target system.

2. Click on the **File** menu and then click on **Add/Remove Snap-in...**.

3. In the **Available Snap-ins** listbox, click on **Certificates** to highlight it and click on the **Add** button to move it to **Selected snap-ins**.

4. In the **Certificates** snap-in dialog, select **Computer account** and click on **Next**.

5. Choose **Local computer** or enter the name or IP address of the target system as necessary. Then, click on **Finish**.

6. Expand **Personal** in the **Certificates** tree. If it has a subfolder named **Certificates**, then this is where the computer's certificates will appear. Verify that at least one of the certificates has not expired and has **Intended Purpose** of **Server Authentication**. Double-click on the certificate. On the **General** tab, verify that you recognize the entity in the **Issued by** field and that you can access it to retrieve the certificate authority chain. If a certificate is present that meets all these requirements, no further certificate work is required on this system, and you can skip the remaining steps. The following screenshot shows a certificate with the proper Server Authentication:

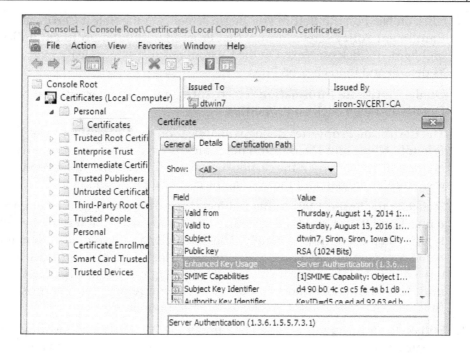

7. If the computer does not have a valid certificate, right-click on **Personal** and hover over **All Tasks**. If you know that this system is joined to a domain with a defined enrollment policy, choose **Request New Certificate** and continue with step 8.

    In any other case, especially if the system that generates the request is not the system that will host the certificate, go to **All Tasks**, then **Advanced Operations**, and click on **Create Custom Request**. Skip to step 11.

8. On the **Certificate Enrollment** page, ensure that a preconfigured policy is highlighted. If none exists, you'll need to cancel the enrollment, go back to step 6, and follow the directions for a custom request in step 7.

9. On the **Request Certificates** page, check whether the certificate template includes **Server Authentication**. The **Computer** and **Web Server** templates satisfy this requirement. Once you have selected a template, perform steps 12-15 to configure it, and then finish with step 10.

10. Click on **Enroll**. You will be returned to the main MMC window and the certificate will automatically appear under the **Certificates** branch. The configuration of this system's certificate is complete and you don't need to follow any more steps. If there are any errors, work with your PKI administrator to address any issues and start again.

11. Click on **Next** on the **Before you Begin** screen. On the **Select Certificate Enrollment Policy** screen, ensure that **Proceed without enrollment policy** is highlighted. Click on **Next**. On the **Custom request** screen, leave everything as default and then click on **Next**.

12. On the **Certificate Information** screen, click on the down-arrow next to **Details** and then click on **Properties**.

13. The **Certificate Properties** dialog will appear on the **General** tab. The **Friendly Name** and **Description** fields are optional. However, **Friendly Name** will appear when the certificate is viewed in a list, so it's a good idea to enter the name of the system the certificate will belong to.

14. Switch to the **Subject** tab. In the **Subject name** dropdown, select **Common name**. Enter the name of the system. This should match the way that you'll type it when connecting remotely. This is usually a fully-qualified domain name, for example, `hv-perim1.siron.int`. It's also standard practice to fill out a number of the other fields, specifically, **Organization, Organization unit, Locality**, and **Country**, but this is not a requirement for Enterprise CAs (if you are using a public CA, check their requirements).

15. Still on the **Subject** tab, choose **DNS** under the **Alternative name** dropdown. Create an entry that matches with what you used for the common name in step 14. Create additional entries for any other method that might be used to connect to this host through PowerShell, such as a short name, fully-qualified aliases, and IP address(es). If you were able to use a predefined policy in step 7, return to step 10 to finish the connection. Otherwise, proceed with step 16.

16. Switch to the **Extensions** tab and expand **Key Usage**. Highlight **Digital signature** under **Available Options** and click on **Add**. Follow suit for **Key encipherment**. Next, expand **Extended Key Usage**. Highlight **Server Authentication** under **Available Options** and click on **Add**.

17. Switch to the **Private Key** tab. Expand **Key options**. To comply with modern cryptographic standards, set the key size to a minimum of `2048`. Be aware that key sizes over `4096` could require a significant amount of processing power and will not meaningfully increase security in this usage. If you are creating this request for a system you are not currently connected to (such as a computer in the perimeter network), check the **Make private key exportable** box.

18. Click on **OK**. Back in the **Certificate Enrollment** screen, click on **Next**. On the next screen, you'll be asked where to save the file and what format to use. For an Active Directory certificate server, use **Base 64**. If you are using another authority, check with their support team. If they use a copy/paste text field for the **certificate signing request (CSR)**, then choose **Base 64**. Click on **Finish**.

19. The final product is a `.req` file. If you saved it in **Base 64**, you can open the file in Notepad. The output should be a garble of text bracketed by **-----BEGIN NEW CERTIFICATE REQUEST-----** and **-----END NEW CERTIFICATE REQUEST-----**, as shown in the following screenshot:

20. If you are using a non-Windows authority, follow their directions to submit the request, retrieve the certificate files once they have been provided to you, and skip to step 25. Otherwise, copy all of the file's contents including the **BEGIN** and **END** text lines to the clipboard and continue with step 21.

21. Access your domain's certificate authority issuing web page. The default is to use a `/CertSrv` virtual directory, so your URL will be something like `https://svcert/CertSrv`. You may be prompted to log in; the account you use will depend on your PKI configuration. Choose an account that has the ability to request certificates.

22. On the **Welcome** screen, click on **Request a certificate**. On the next page, click on **advanced certificate request**. On the following page, click on **Submit a certificate request by using a base-64-encoded CMC or PKCS #10 file, or submit a renewal request by using a base-64-encoded PKCS #7 file**.

23. Paste the text of the CSR file into the large textbox in the **Saved Request** section. Under **Certificate Template**, choose **Web Server** (or another template that contains the Server Authentication usage). Click on **Submit**.

24. Leave the **DER encoded** selection and click on **Download certificate**. Save the file (change the name and location if you wish). Use the **Download certificate chain** link as well as this will be needed later.

25. Return to the Certificates MMC console. Right-click on **Personal**, hover over **All Tasks**, and click on **Import**. Click on **Next** on the **Welcome** screen. On the **File to Import** screen, locate the file you downloaded in the previous step (or from the provider, if using a third party) and then click on **Next**. Make sure that the selected store is **Personal**. Click on **Next** and then on **Finish**. Verify that the certificate is as requested. Use the screenshot from step 6 as a comparison. If the system that the console is connected to is the system that needs the certificate, then its configuration is complete and you don't need to follow any more steps. If the certificate is meant for another computer, continue from step 26.

26. Document the expiration date of the newly created certificate, setting a reminder to renew it prior to expiration. Right-click on it and hover over **All Tasks**, then click on **Export....**. Click on **Next** on the **Welcome** screen.

27. Choose **Yes, export the private key**. If this option is not available, then you either did not set the option to mark the key as exportable in step 17 or you did not choose the custom option in step 7. In either case, this key is not usable and you'll need to start over. If you are able to export the private key, click on **Next**.

28. On the **Export File Format** screen, the only available selection should be **Personal Information Exchange – PKCS #12 (.PFX)**. If any of the options above that are selectable, return to the previous screen and ensure that **Yes, export the private key** is selected. Click on **Next**.

29. Create a password you can remember and enter it in both fields. Click on **Next**. Choose a filename and click on **Next**. Finally, click on **Finish**.

30. Transfer the `.pfx` file that was created in step 29 to the target system (this example will use a file named `perimeterbox.pfx` in a folder named `C:\Certfiles`). In a command prompt, enter the following:

```
Certutil.exe -ImportPFX C:\Certfiles\perimeterbox.pfx
```

31. As a best practice, delete the certificate from the system that generated it. Do this by right-clicking on it in the **Certificates** tree and clicking on **Delete**. Delete any exported certificate files as well. This will not affect the validity of the certificate that you imported on the target system.

Once all the preceding steps have completed, the target system has a valid certificate that it can use to encrypt communications to clients that request it. As previously mentioned, this certificate will appear under the **Personal** branch of the **Certificates** tree when you are viewing computer certificates. It should also have a certificate for the certificate authority that generated the certificate. Verify that by looking under the **Trusted Root Certification Authorities** branch. If the system doesn't have a GUI, you can verify the certificates by running the following in the command prompt:

```
certutil -viewstore My
certutil -viewstore Root
```

If you received a certificate from a public authority and they utilize Intermediate certificates, look in store CA instead of Root. If the proper root certificate is missing, read the following subsection for directions.

Before you can connect systems remotely, you need to tell WinRM to listen for secure connections and you need to adjust the firewall. Both of these steps are simple. For WinRM, open an elevated prompt and type the following:

```
winrm quickconfig -transport:https
```

 These instructions set up a basic WinRM listener that works with the default certificate on the current computer name. If you'd like to use an alternate certificate or hostname, further instructions are available on the TechNet site at http://technet.microsoft.com/en-us/library/cc782312(v=WS.10).aspx.

For the firewall, you can use the Windows Firewall with Advanced Security applet in **Administrative Tools** to create a new rule that opens port 5986. Remember to leverage options such as those on the **Scope** tab to restrict inbound connections. As PowerShell Remoting is already restricted to members of the local Administrators group, it is usually not necessary to set further restrictions using the firewall policies. For automation purposes, or for systems that don't have a GUI, you can accomplish the same thing in PowerShell:

```
New-NetFirewallRule -Name "WinRM-SSL-In" -DisplayName "WinRM over HTTPS"
-Description "Allow PowerShell Remoting using HTTPS" -Group "Windows
Management Instrumentation (WMI)" -Enabled True -Profile Any -Direction
Inbound -Action Allow -Protocol TCP -LocalPort 5986 -RemoteAddress
192.168.25.50-192.168.25.125, 10.10.10.20
```

The preceding command looks complicated, but not all of these fields are mandatory. The required parameters are Name, Enabled, Profile, Direction, Action, Protocol, and LocalPort. The rest, and any others you would like to use, are optional. There are other possibilities in the Windows Firewall that allow you to further restrict incoming communications. Research them using the applet's help system or Get-Help.

Configuring the Remote System

When you are using SSL for PowerShell Remoting, the host will present a certificate to the connecting clients. If the client doesn't trust the certificate authority that issued the certificate, the connection will fail. If the connecting system is a member of the domain that issued the certificate, or if the certificate was issued by a well-known public authority, then you likely need to do nothing else. For any other scenario, you need to import the root certificate into the connecting computer.

Before you begin investigating certificates, remember that the remote system also needs to be configured for PowerShell Remoting. At an elevated PowerShell prompt, enter the following:

```
Enable-PSRemoting -Force
```

If the system is a full GUI copy of Windows or it is possible to connect to it from a GUI installation, follow steps 1-5 in the previous section to open the Certificates MMC snap-in. Expand the **Trusted Root Certification Authorities** branch and look for a certificate that pertains to the authority that signed the certificate on the host. On any system, such as one without a GUI, you can also run the following at an elevated command prompt:

```
certutil -viewstore Root
```

For some public authorities, you may need to look in CA instead of Root. If the certificate is not present, you'll first need to acquire it. If you followed all the steps in the previous section, step 24 instructed you to export the certificate chain. This should have presented you with a .p7b file. If you did not get this file, getting a new one depends on the root authority that you used. If it's a public authority, follow their directions to retrieve a certificate chain. For an Active Directory certificate server, access your certificate server's web enrollment page, which will have a URL something like https://svcert/CertSrv. On its main page, click on **Download a CA certificate, certificate chain**, or **CRL**. Click on **Yes** in the dialog and then click on the link **Download CA certificate chain**. This will save a file named certnew.p7b to your local system.

Once you have this file, you can import it into the Certificates MMC snap-in using step 25 of the directions in the previous section. You can also import it with the following command:

```
certutil -importcert Root certnew.p7b
```

If your file came from a public authority, use the name of the file that you downloaded. If the authority indicated that it should be imported into the `Intermediate` store, use `CA` instead of `Root`.

 If you are unable to import the certificate, you can set `-SkipCACheck` in a `PSSessionOption` object passed to the `-SessionOption` parameter of `Enter-PSSession` and `Invoke-Command`, although this lowers security as you cannot be certain of the host's certificate status. See the following URL for information on creating this object: `http://technet.microsoft.com/en-us/library/hh849703.aspx`.

TrustedHosts-based PowerShell Remoting

As an alternative to using SSL for PowerShell Remoting, you can configure TrustedHosts. This procedure must be performed on remote and host systems.

To configure a host named `SVHV1` to allow connections from remote systems named `DESKTOP1` and `LAPTOP4`, enter the following in an elevated command prompt on `SVHV1`:

```
winrm set winrm/config/client @{TrustedHosts="DESKTOP1,LAPTOP1"}
```

On each of the two named remote systems, this command must be entered:

```
winrm set winrm/config/client @{TrustedHosts="SVHV1"}
```

If the connection will be made using the FQDN of the host or if you want the option to use its short name or its FQDN, you can enter them like this:

```
winrm set winrm/config/client @{TrustedHosts="SVHV1,svhv1.siron.int"}
```

The names to be used must match exactly on both ends or connections will fail. Also, using only the preceding commands, modifications to the TrustedHosts list require you to re-enter all current entries. You can view them with the following command:

```
winrm get winrm/config/client
```

PowerShell MVP Jeffery Hicks has written a tutorial on working with the TrustedHosts list that makes complicated manipulations easier. You can view it at the following URL: `http://mcpmag.com/articles/2010/03/30/trusted-host.aspx`.

Choosing between SSL and TrustedHosts

At first glance, the TrustedHosts options may seem preferable. They require far fewer steps to implement and are therefore somewhat easier to understand. If no PKI is available, they may be the only choice. However, when PKI is available, the usage of SSL is preferable for these reasons:

- TrustedHosts performs no computer authentication of any kind. If a connecting computer presents a name that is on the trusted list, it is accepted without further verification. These names are exchanged on initial connection, so even though communications are encrypted, it would be possible to intercept the message.

- SSL requires that the connecting machine trust the certificate issuer. Without opening up your PKI unnecessarily, this is only possible for domain guests. Even if a system has somehow managed to retrieve a certificate, it has a built-in expiration date. The TrustedHosts list does not expire.

- If a PKI is already in place, documentation is likely to be already handled. As a result, maintenance is much simpler than tracking the settings for TrustedHosts across multiple systems.

Even though the SSL instructions look long and complicated, following them through to completion should take no more than a few minutes.

 When making your decision, encryption is not a meaningful factor. WSMan traffic is always encrypted. The SSL option is only for the usage of certificates.

Example – PowerShell Remoting with Invoke-Command

You'll find that PowerShell Remoting using `Enter-PSSession` is quite simple and straightforward. `Invoke-Command` can take a bit longer to get used to. The following example connects to two Hyper-V hosts, determines which guests are stopped, starts them, and returns their names to the calling system. Notice the use of the ScriptBlock variable to hold the set of commands that we want to run.

```
$TargetSystems = "svhv1", "svhv2"
$ScriptBlock = {
  $StoppedStates = "Off", "Saved"
  $StoppedVMs = Get-VM | where { $_.State -in $StoppedStates }
  $StoppedVMs | Start-VM
```

```
    $StoppedVMs | select Name
}
Invoke-Command -ComputerName $TargetSystems -Credential
(Get-Credential) -ScriptBlock $ScriptBlock
```

Because we did not use the `HideComputerName` parameter of `Invoke-Command`, the output of the preceding script will include the name of the host along with the name of each virtual machine that was started.

Using custom PowerShell Remoting endpoints

While the ability to operate directly at a remote PowerShell prompt is certainly an enticing reason to use PowerShell Remoting, the benefits don't stop there. Only members of the host's local Administrators group are allowed to connect using the direct methods displayed so far. However, with a little effort, you can design custom endpoints and delegate their usage to anyone as necessary.

You begin by defining the capabilities of the endpoint. This is done with the `New-PSSessionConfigurationFile` cmdlet, which, as its name implies, creates a file that lays out the structure of the endpoint. A sample usage of this cmdlet is shown as follows:

```
New-PSSessionConfigurationFile -Path C:\Scripts\GetVM.pssc -SessionType
RestrictedRemoteServer -ModulesToImport HyperV -VisibleCmdlets Get-VM
-VisibleFunctions Get-VM -LanguageMode NoLanguage
```

With this, we have created a descriptor file for a custom endpoint that can't do anything but run the `Get-VM` cmdlet. The file is saved as `GetVM.pscc` in the `C:\Scripts` folder on the Hyper-V host. To continue our sample, we have created a global security group in the domain named `Hyper-V Viewers`. To this group, we have added a domain user account named `HVViewer`. This user is not in any other security group, not even Hyper-V Administrators. Next, we create the endpoint from the file as follows:

```
Register-PSSessionConfiguration -Name GetVMOnly -RunAsCredential (Get-
Credential) -ShowSecurityDescriptorUI -Path C:\Scripts\GetVM.pssc
```

On submitting this cmdlet, you'll first be prompted for credentials, with a warning displayed in the background. The credentials that you supply must have the capability to run the cmdlets you allowed in the configuration file, but they don't necessarily need to be an administrator. The warning lets you know that because the session will run as those credentials, there won't be any way to distinguish who exactly is submitting commands in the session, so you need to take care to lock down the session appropriately. You will then be prompted to set up the session. After that, you'll be asked to fill in a security dialog. This is the result of the -ShowSecurityDescriptorUI parameter, which we're using so that we don't have to manually enter the fairly complex security descriptor syntax. What you're being asked for is to fill out the security of the endpoint itself. In our case, we'll add the security group that we created for this purpose and grant it **Execute (Invoke)** permissions. This is shown in the following screenshot:

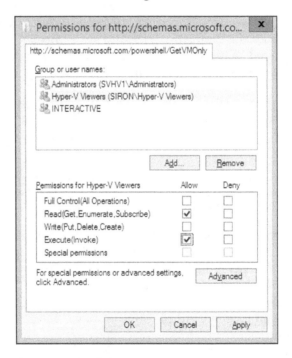

Everything is prepared. To connect to this endpoint, use the following:

```
Enter-PSSession -ComputerName svhv1 -Credential (Get-Credential)
-ConfigurationName GetVMOnly
```

When prompted, you can use a security account in the **Hyper-V Viewers** group. It will be running as the account specified when you registered the session, but it will not be able to run anything at all except Get-VM.

Practical custom PowerShell Remoting endpoints

To reiterate one of the key points of the session created in the previous section, the security groups allowed for connecting to the custom endpoint have no security privileges on the Hyper-V host at all. They are only allowed to access the session. This opens up a great deal of power to delegates who can perform specific functions.

In this day and age of the private and hybrid clouds, you might be serving as the administrator for a Hyper-V host that is running a number of operating system environments with their own administrators. You may want to grant them the ability to restart their own virtual machines and nothing else. To simulate this, we've taken the file generated by the New-PSSessionConfigurationFile in the previous section and copied it to a new file named OperateMyVM.pssc. We've edited this file so that VisibleAliases, VisibleCmdlets, and VisibleFunctions are set to an empty pair of single-quote marks (' '). We then modified FunctionDefinitions so that it looks like the following:

```
FunctionDefinitions = @(
@{
  Name='Stop-MyVM'
  Options='ReadOnly'
  ScriptBlock={ Stop-VM -Name svmyvm -Force }
}
@{
  Name='Start-MyVM'
  Options='ReadOnly'
  ScriptBlock={ Start-VM -Name svmyvm }
}
@{
  Name='Get-MyVM'
  Options='ReadOnly'
  ScriptBlock={ Get-VM -Name svmyvm }
}
)
```

Finally, we registered it as a session on the Hyper-V host:

```
Register-PSSessionConfiguration -Name OperateMyVM -RunAsCredential
(Get-Credential) -ShowSecurityDescriptorUI -Path C:\Scripts\OperateMyVM.
pssc
```

Users who connect to this endpoint will be able to run the functions that you defined: `Get-MyVM`, `Stop-MyVM`, and `Start-MyVM`. They won't be able to do anything else. Using custom endpoints like this can serve as a replacement for the older **Authorization Manager (AzMan)** technology. AzMan was deprecated in 2012 and removed in 2012 R2. It is recommended that anyone still using this technology should transition to alternate solutions such as those presented in this chapter.

Summary

This chapter was dedicated to the topic of securing virtual machines from their host. We started with a look at the built-in Hyper-V Administrators group and how it is managed. Next, you learned how to configure PowerShell Remoting for a number of scenarios and how to use it to control access over virtual machines.

The purpose of this chapter was to illustrate how to defend your virtual machines from unauthorized access through the hypervisor. In the next chapter, we'll talk about the feasibility of securing virtual machines from the same context that we would secure physical machines.

4
Securing Virtual Machines

Until now, we focused on the host and hypervisor. Virtual machines (VMs) run a complete operating system, usually attached to the network, and are presented to the rest of the world in much the same way as a physical machine would be. With the built-in isolation of the guest from its host, it's impossible for the hypervisor to provide multiple intercessions on behalf of the virtual machine. In this chapter, we will talk about the ways in which virtual machines are—and are not—special in terms of security.

In this chapter, you will learn about:

- Understanding the security environment of virtual machines
- Leveraging Generation 2 virtual machines
- Employing anti-malware on a virtual machine
- Considering intrusion prevention and detection strategies
- Using Group Policy with virtual machines
- Limiting exposure through resource restrictions
- Applying general best practices

Understanding the security environment of VMs

Understanding the security needs of a virtual machine depends on the depth of understanding how virtual machines operate. For a great many administrators, the way that hypervisors and their guests interoperate is nearly a complete mystery. Many of the explanatory documents treat this subject with highly detailed architecture terminology that is often confusing and more than a few administrators want or need to know.

The primary feature of hypervisor terminology is **isolation**. Even though management operating systems and all of its guests share a hardware environment, the central purpose of the hypervisor is to create separate environments that are prevented from interfering with each other. While it is usually not a surprise to anyone that guests are walled off from each other, it may not be obvious that the management operating system also lacks direct access to the guests. This can sometimes serve as a point of frustration as administrators often have a legitimate need to move data directly between the management operating system and a guest. However, any such mechanism is relatively easy for an attacker to exploit. Therefore, isolation is the rule.

Even with isolation being the goal, the unavoidable truth is that the management operating system and all its guests share a single set of hardware. It's helpful to have some understanding of how Hyper-V controls hardware access.

Process isolation

All virtual machines need access to at least a single physical CPU core. Hyper-V does not assign physical cores directly to guests. Instead, it uses an algorithm that tries to evenly distribute the processing load across available hardware in such a way that any CPU core could be running a thread from any given virtual machine at any time.

Hyper-V handles these threads in much the same fashion that the Windows operating system uses to manage threads from running processes. The guest operating systems run processes just as they would in a nonvirtualized environment. By running on a higher **privilege level** (known as a **ring**) on the physical CPUs, Hyper-V is able to directly manage all threads from all guests.

> The privilege level, or ring, where standard operating systems run is ring 0. Hardware-assisted virtualization technologies provided by advanced CPUs make a higher privilege level available, known as ring -1. This is where Hyper-V runs.

Because Hyper-V manages all threads at this level, it is not necessary for guest threads to pass through the management operating system. Therefore, a **break-out attack** (an attack that crosses isolation boundaries) at the process level is not any more likely to occur from the management operating system than from a guest. Attacks of this nature are heavily mitigated by technologies such as CPU-based hardware-assisted virtualization and **data execution prevention** (**DEP**), both of which are required to run Hyper-V. Other mitigation strategies can be effectively handled by other common techniques, which will be brought up later in this chapter.

Memory isolation

For the most part, memory isolation occurs naturally along with process isolation following the same rules. Processes own specific ranges of memory. Operating systems are aware of which memory is owned by which process, for example, Hyper-V is aware of which memory is owned by which virtual machine. A **memory access violation** occurs when a process attempts to perform an action on memory that it does not own. These violations are almost exclusively the results of errors, not malicious attacks. They are so common that modern operating systems and hypervisors already employ a great deal of protection against them. Ordinarily, a memory access violation will result in the offending process being denied and in extreme cases, terminated.

Of course, as the arbiter of memory ownership, the operating system can access any memory. A number of attack methods exist that are designed to leverage this fact in order to gain access to or control over processes, or to break out of standard processes into the operating system. These attacks are naturally mitigated by technologies such as DEP and **address space layout randomization (ASLR)**. ASLR is specifically meant to protect the operating system, as many critical components have historically been placed in well-known locations. ASLR scrambles these so that they will not be predictable from one instance of the operating system to the next.

Hyper-V virtualizes the memory used by guests. Like process isolation, memory access does not need to be brokered by the management operating system. The physical locations of all guests' memory are known only to Hyper-V and cannot be ascertained by compromising the management operating system. This serves as a form of ASLR. Therefore, a successful memory break-out attack is most likely to cause memory corruption in an unpredictable location. Due to the previously mentioned mitigation factors, such an attack is extremely unlikely. What is much more likely is a **denial-of-service (DoS)** attack. An attack of this type will continuously attempt to access memory that it is not authorized to and continually will be denied by Hyper-V, but at such a high rate that it impacts the performance of other virtual machines. We will discuss mitigation approaches later in this chapter.

Hard disk isolation

Unlike CPUs and memory, virtual machines access to hard disks must be routed through the management operating system. It is the combined job of the management operating system and Hyper-V to ensure that virtual machines only access data that they are allowed to. However, a compromise of the management operating system would instantly place the storage of all virtual machines at risk. A break-out attack on storage from within a virtual machine will face the same trials as a memory break-out attack; it will be serious but far more likely to cause unspecified damage than to allow a targeted retrieval of sensitive information. We will pay much more attention to the subject of storage security in *Chapter 6, Securing Hyper-V Storage*.

Network isolation

Networking works much differently than the previously discussed technologies. Isolation must occur at two levels: the virtual switch and the virtual adapter. Also, a virtual adapter can be paravirtualized, emulated, or using **single-root I/O virtualization (SR-IOV)**, it can bypass the hypervisor entirely. *Chapter 5, Securing the Network,* is all about networking security in Hyper-V.

Other hardware

The rest of the hardware that can be used by virtual machines works on a model similar to the virtual network adapter. It can be **emulated**, under which the hypervisor creates a hardware construct that acts like a particular physical device. The common examples are the legacy virtual network adapter and IDE drives, although some minor system component hardware is also virtualized. The other type is paravirtualized, or **synthetic** hardware. For this type, Hyper-V presents an interface directly to the guest that allows it to work through a high-performance I/O system called **VMBus**. Usage of this bus requires the guest to be **enlightened**. This is accomplished through the presence of specialized software called **integration components** in the guest that makes its operating system aware of VMBus. Generally, none of this presents any particular security issue that makes one type preferable to the other. However, VMBus is not available to non-enlightened guests, so they will escape any compromise of that subsystem. At the same time, emulated hardware is exposed to guests through vmwp.exe in the management operating system, so all guests are at risk from attacks on that component.

Practical approaches to isolation security

For the most part, knowledge of the preceding section is almost exclusively educational and should be of little concern. As of now, there has been only one known compromise in these systems. This was published in *Microsoft Security Bulletin MS13-092,* which you can read at https://technet.microsoft.com/en-us/library/security/ms13-092.aspx. The vulnerability was addressed in a patch, as indicated by the bulletin.

Other known vulnerabilities of the hypervisor have been addressed, but the worst only allowed DoS attacks. None were as serious as MS13-092. However, there is a lack of information on the volume of attempts made on Hyper-V. By all evidence, it appears that the management operating system and guest operating systems continue to be the most common target for attackers. While the complexity of the hypervisor alone means that it's likely to have some security flaws, spending much time to focus on securing the hypervisor components is not likely to be a worthwhile endeavor.

Leveraging Generation 2 virtual machines

A new feature of Hyper-V in the 2012 R2 series is **Generation 2 virtual machines**. While the traditional virtual machine uses an emulated BIOS, these make use of the newer, more efficient and robust **Unified Extensible Firmware Interface (UEFI)** model. The greatest benefit of using these virtual machines is quicker boot up times. They don't offer a great deal more than that and almost nothing in terms of security. A Generation 2 virtual machine doesn't use emulated hardware, so a compromise of vmwp.exe would theoretically have less impact on a Generation 2 guest. However, the likelihood of such a compromise is so low that this is of little concern.

What the Generation 2 VM does offer in terms of security is **Secure Boot**. Secure Boot is an agreement between the firmware and the boot image whether it is a DVD, hard drive file, or PXE image. This is handled by a PKI configuration in which the firmware can recognize the digital signatures presented by the boot system. If those keys aren't present or are not valid, the boot process fails. Using this mechanism, systems whose boot images have been modified by malware such as root kits will fail to even start.

Secure Boot requires no special hardware, places no particular burden on the host or guest, and should be employed wherever it is applicable. Unfortunately, its range of applicability is currently limited. Only 2012 R2 or later hosts can operate Generation 2 virtual machines. The only guest operating systems eligible for Secure Boot on this platform are Windows desktop operating systems Version 8 and later and server operating systems Versions 2012 and later. As of the time of this writing, no non-Microsoft operating system operates as a Secure Boot Hyper-V guest. Later versions will add support for other guest operating systems.

Secure Boot should be enabled by default on all Generation 2 virtual machines, so you shouldn't need to do anything. Changing the Secure Boot settings is very simple. While the Generation 2 machine you wish to change is turned off, open its **Settings** dialog and switch to the **Firmware** tab. Check or clear the box for Secure Boot as desired. This is shown in the following screenshot:

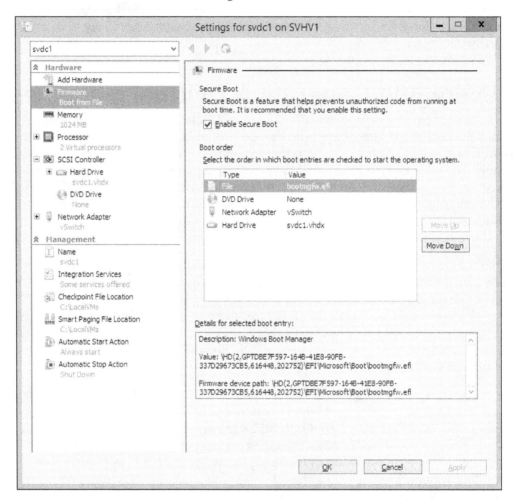

Secure Boot can also be set simply from PowerShell (again, the VM must be turned off) by executing the following command:

```
Set-VMFirmware -VMName svdc1 -EnableSecureBoot On
```

Employing anti-malware on a virtual machine

While the value of using anti-malware in the parent partition is generally frowned upon due to performance concerns, and while there is the possibility of inadvertently damaging guest files, there is no such concern when it comes to the guests. Because the guests run all types of software, they automatically have a much greater attack surface than the management operating system.

The potential negative reach of anti-malware in the guest is limited. Anywhere that such software is employed, there is a concern that it might detect a **false positive**. This happens when anti-malware incorrectly classifies safe, official software as a threat. The software will then take some action to mitigate this threat, and in the case of a false positive, this can be highly disruptive to operations.

When such a false positive occurs in the management operating system, every single virtual machine could be a victim. The reason why this is more of a concern at the management operating system layer is that by nature, hypervisors perform suspicious activities, such as controlling memory and I/O access for other processes. As a general rule, guests should not engage in such activities, so the risk of a false positive at these levels can be substantially lower.

Usage of anti-malware inside guests can automatically provide a layer of protection for the management operating system. Because virtual machines are the most likely parts of the virtualized environment to be exposed to attackers, they are the most likely entry point for any attacks on the hypervisor. Anti-malware in the guests can help block such attacks.

Considering intrusion prevention and detection strategies

Anti-malware serves the purpose of detection and treatment of malicious software, but it is not the only available option. There is a great quantity of available options for intrusion detection and prevention. The selection is so wide that just about any security software that doesn't immediately qualify as anti-malware falls into this category.

For instance, the Microsoft Baseline Security Analyzer that we talked about in *Chapter 3, Securing Virtual Machines from the Hypervisor,* can qualify as intrusion prevention software. This software is used to remotely scan a system for known vulnerabilities and generate a report. Unlike anti-malware applications, it is left up to you to address any concerns. Because this type of software does not run constantly, it can be scheduled for times when its system impact is minimal. You are highly encouraged to employ a solution in this genre.

Intrusion detection software is almost always much more invasive. It often works by establishing a baseline, essentially a pattern of normal usage. When an activity deviates from this baseline, it is reported, and optionally countered. Unlike standard anti-malware, it usually does not rely heavily on patterns developed by the software manufacturer.

Usage of intrusion detection software often requires a fair amount of overhead on the part of systems administrators. Logs must be monitored and maintained; probable intrusions must be investigated. If there is no one available to perform these tasks, the software might simply be placing a load on your systems without giving any meaningful benefit. Ensure that if you are going to employ such a solution, your organization is actually going to make use of it.

Using Group Policy with virtual machines

For the most part, Group Policy assignments for virtual machines are not performed differently than how they would have been performed if the systems were installed directly on physical hardware. Depending on the structure of your Active Directory, they might wind up in Organizational Units alongside physical deployments. As an example, you may have Windows 7 computers that are part of a **virtual desktop infrastructure (VDI)**. For these, you can restrict who can log in remotely, but otherwise you might want them to have the same policies as regular Windows 7 computers. To achieve this, there is an attribute of the virtual machine that can be discovered through **Windows Management Instrumentation (WMI)** and filtered in Group Policy.

To restrict Group Policy to virtual machines, execute the following steps:

1. Open Group Policy Management Console. Right-click on **WMI Filters** in the tree and click on **New**. Give it an identifiable name; these steps can be used on virtual machines only.

2. Click on **Add**. In the WMI Query dialog box, enter **Namespace** as `root\CIMv2`. In the Query textbox, enter the following:

    ```
    SELECT * FROM Win32_ComputerSystem WHERE Model = "Virtual Machine"
    ```

3. Click on **OK**. You might receive a warning that the namespace is not valid. Click on **OK** to that if it appears. Back in the **New WMI Filter** dialog, click on **Save**.

4. Create a new GPO, and optionally link it to the destination OU (these instructions won't remind you again). Once the policy is created, edit it, and set the desired options.

5. Highlight the policy in the tree (either on the actual GPO or one of its links). At the bottom of the information pane is a **WMI Filtering** section. Use the drop-down box to select the WMI filter you created in step 1. You will be prompted to confirm that you wish to use this filter. Once you click on **Yes**, the filter will be immediately applied. A screenshot of this is as follows:

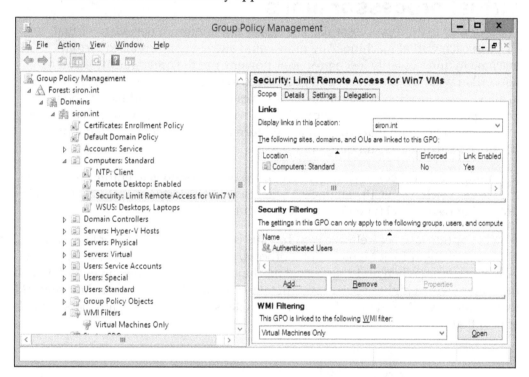

 Despite its name, this filter does not apply to all possible virtual machines but only to Windows computers that are Hyper-V guests.

Limiting exposure with resource limitations

As explained earlier in this chapter, the purpose of a denial-of-service attack is to force a system to devote so many resources to dealing with an attack that it has little or nothing left over for legitimate purposes. Like most hypervisors, Hyper-V does a good job of maintaining resource balance so that such attacks are rarely more than a nuisance. There are a number of steps you can take to preemptively constrain the impact of such attacks.

Virtual processor limits

The best way to limit processor use is to apply the minimum necessary virtual CPUs to each virtual machine. Any more could allow a compromised virtual machine to unnecessarily leech processor power from the other guests. If you're not certain what the minimum is, a good place to start is with two. This is enough to allow an application to dominate CPU cycles while still providing a responsive guest operating system. Application vendors will often provide you with a desired minimum. Other than that, you can use Performance Monitor or another tool to perform trend analysis and determine a reasonable minimum.

If limiting the vCPU count is not sufficient, the other option is to enforce fixed limits. If a virtual machine's vCPU attempts to exceed a particular percentage of the host's processing resources, Hyper-V's thread scheduler will throttle it.

Another option is to set **Relative weight**. This is roughly the equivalent of setting a process priority in Task Manager for a process, except that this applies to the entire virtual machine. When multiple virtual machines request CPU resources at the same time, those with a higher relative weight take priority. Hyper-V won't allow any VM to completely starve out of CPU time, but in a dense system with many tiers, it might appear that way.

These options are set on the virtual machine's **Processor** tab, as shown in the following screenshot:

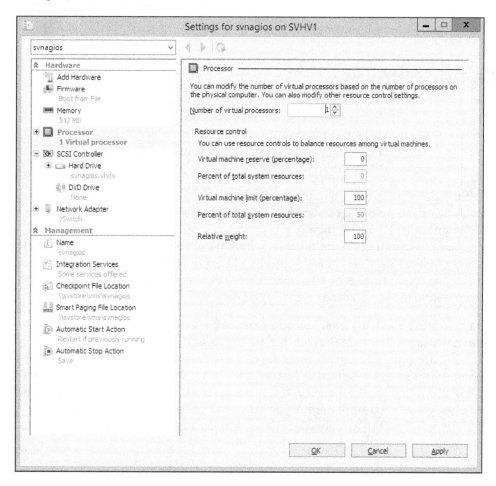

The number that you can modify is **Virtual machine limit (percentage)**. This sets the maximum percentage of its allocated vCPUs that the virtual machine is allowed to use. The combination of this field and **Number of virtual processors** will automatically be used to calculate the **Percent of total system resources** value. In the preceding screenshot, 100 percent of a single vCPU is allowed for a virtual machine that is on a dual-core host. This amounts to a maximum of 50 percent of the total processing resources. The same setting on a quad-core host would result in a 25 percent cap.

The options can also be set through PowerShell, as follows:

```
Set-VMProcessor -VMName svnagios -Count 1 -Maximum 50 -RelativeWeight 100
```

The relative weight is a minimum of 0 and a maximum of 10,000. The default is 100.

Memory limits

As with CPU limits, the best way to limit memory usage is through careful provisioning. Unlike other hypervisors, Hyper-V does not overcommit memory. Therefore, it is more difficult for a compromised virtual machine to cause memory starvation to others. However, injudicious Dynamic Memory settings could lead to a potential issue with contention.

Part of the problem is that Dynamic Memory defaults to a 1 terabyte upper limit. If not changed, all guests set to use Dynamic Memory will have the same upper limit. When under demand, memory is allocated to guests on a first-come, first-served basis, depending on memory weight. Unless your host has over 1 terabyte of installed physical RAM, Hyper-V could be placed in a position in which it is unable to satisfy the requirements of all guests. In addition to cramping running VMs, it is not be possible to start any that are stopped or saved.

Begin by setting all virtual machines to reasonable maximums. Follow the sizing guides of the application manufacturer as well as any suggestions that you can glean from trend analysis. Remember that you can always adjust the Dynamic Memory maximum upward, even while the guest is running, so you should be able to start low and add memory as necessary. If it is not possible to reasonably limit a high-risk guest through its maximum memory setting, you can also lower its memory weight. Both settings are on the **Memory** tab, as seen in the following screenshot:

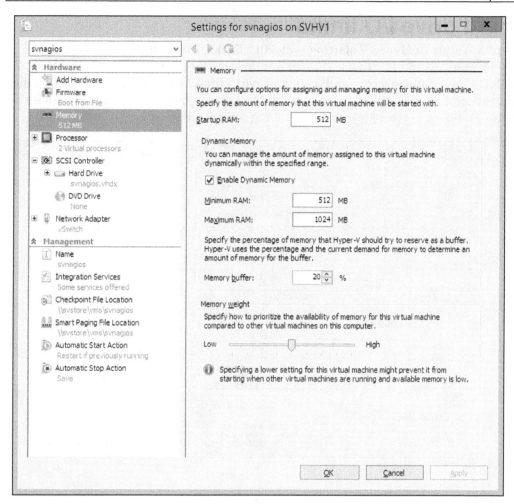

To set the limits through PowerShell, execute the following command:

```
Set-VMMemory -VMName svdc1 -MaximumBytes 1GB -Priority 50
```

In PowerShell, the priority parameter refers to the weight and accepts values from 0 to 100.

Hard drive I/O limits

A new feature of Hyper-V starting with 2012 R2 is I/O **Quality of Service (QoS)**. While many would like to use it to set minimums, this is difficult for Hyper-V to enforce, especially in a cluster. It can, however, enforce the maximum. It's set on the **Advanced Features** sub-tab of the virtual hard drive's tab in the virtual machine's settings dialog. Have a look at the following screenshot:

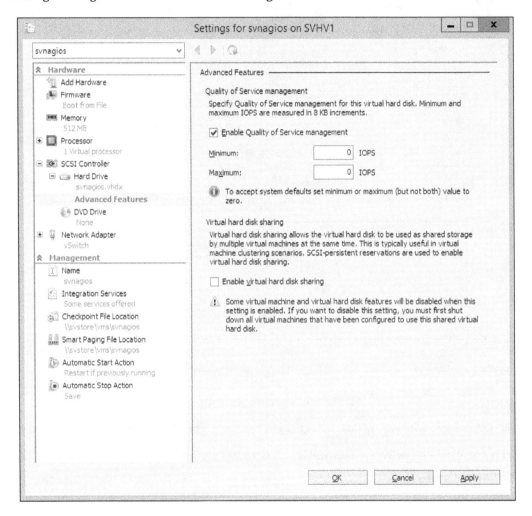

To set the limit in PowerShell, execute the following command:

```
Set-VMHardDiskDrive -VMName svcert -ControllerType SCSI -ControllerNumber
0 -ControllerLocation 0 -MaximumIOPS 10
```

 All settings are in 8-kilobit increments.

You can change these limits at any time.

Virtual network limits

There is a wide variety of options available to restrict and shape virtual network adapter traffic. We will spend some time exploring these in *Chapter 5, Securing the Network*.

Applying general best practices

Protecting virtual machines using Hyper-V's tools is only the beginning. Virtual machines are computers and need to be secured like computers. The following is a list of some common best practices:

- **Control access**: Only allow users with an identified need to access resources on a virtual machine. This includes service points, such as web services, as well as administrative points, such as RDP. For users that do have access, restrict privilege levels to be no more than what is necessary. Even if you trust your users not to engage in malicious behavior, their sessions could be hijacked by software or attackers.

- **Stay logged off**: Do not attach to RDP or PowerShell sessions on virtual machines and then leave them in a disconnected or idle state. In addition to consuming unnecessary resources, it is easier for an attacker to compromise an existing session than to create a new one.

- **Monitor usage**: Monitoring involves auditing both resource access and resource utilization. A high number of failed logons can indicate attempts at a brute-force compromise. Successful logons during strange periods can indicate password theft. Unusually high resource utilization can indicate a breach or a DoS attack.

- **Periodically review access policies**: There's nothing uncommon about employees leaving the organization or switching roles within. Even if there are defined policies that dictate certain security-related activities be performed along with one of these events, it is still highly recommended that security access be periodically reviewed on all systems. This would also include validating what data and resources are exposed to which user groups.

- **Stay current**: For Windows guests, Windows Updates should be configured to run on a schedule. Other operating systems should use automated patching tools as well. Third-party software must be routinely updated. It is best to adopt a hard policy that mandates regular patching of all systems; a companion policy should state that any mission-critical services that are intolerant of downtimes must be architected with some form of failover mechanism in order to be viable for organizational use. It's certainly understood that users are highly displeased by business-interrupting patch cycles, but the 5 to 15 minutes necessary for a virtual machine reboot are insignificant compared to the downtime necessary to seal and recover from a security breach.

Summary

In this chapter, we focused on guest security, both at the virtual machine level and as standard operating systems. We started with an explanation of the way that Hyper-V naturally separates virtual machines into their own environments. Next, we saw the enhanced security option of Secure Boot available to Generation 2 virtual machines. After that, we talked about anti-malware and intrusion detection/prevention software. We also covered how to design Group Policies that only apply to Hyper-V guests. We then talked about the ways to limit resource utilization of a virtual machine so that its maximum impact is reduced. We concluded by listing some generic security best practices to apply to virtual machines.

In the next chapter, we'll look at ways to secure the networking layer in a Hyper-V environment.

5
Securing the Network

Out of all the potential threats to your virtual machines, over-the-network attacks will be the most probable. However, you'll have to accept some level of risk in order for your guests to be able to provide services to network-based clients. Fortunately, there are a number of methods available for you to mitigate those risks to a manageable level.

In this chapter, we'll discuss the following:

- Understanding SSL encryption
- Leveraging network hardware
- Using the Hyper-V virtual switch's isolation technologies
- Employing Hyper-V virtual switch ACLs
- Configuring the Windows Firewall
- Using management tools remotely
- Using Hyper-V with IPsec
- Configuring virtual network adapter protections
- Securing Hyper-V Replica traffic

Understanding SSL encryption

A major flaw has been discovered that allows attackers to easily decipher traffic encrypted with the **Secure Sockets Layer** (**SSL**) 3.0 protocol. This attack is known as **Browser Exploit Against SSL/TLS** (**BEAST**). When perusing the list of available protocols, SSL 3.0 is listed as the highest version with that name, which might give the impression that there are no safe SSL protocols to use.

However, **Transport Layer Security (TLS)** has supplanted these earlier protocols. TLS 1.0 was the successor to SSL 3.0, and in turn, it has been followed by TLS 1.1 and 1.2. When current Windows systems use a certificate-based communications channel, they will use the most secure protocol that is present and enabled on both endpoints. These are often named SSL connections, which can imply that they are using SSL instead of TLS. In truth, Windows certificate-based communications are controlled by the **Schannel** authentication package.

TLS 1.1 and 1.2 are not vulnerable to BEAST, so it is recommended that, at a minimum, these protocols be enabled. It is also possible to disable down-level protocols to prevent Schannel from negotiating with them. One quick method for doing this is by setting the Group Policy option to **System cryptography: Use FIPS compliant algorithms for encryption, hashing, and signing**. For instructions on working with policies, refer to the *Leveraging Group Policy* section of *Chapter 2, Securing the Host*. This particular policy is located under **Computer Configuration | Policies | Windows Settings | Security Options**.

> Requiring FIPS-compliant algorithms may break third-party applications. Test thoroughly prior to implementing this setting in a production environment.

Be aware that the FIPS setting, by itself, only disables SSL protocols. TLS 1.0 is still enabled, and it is vulnerable to BEAST. You can exercise more precise control over which protocols are enabled by following the instructions in Microsoft's knowledge article *KB245030* at `http://support.microsoft.com/kb/245030`.

Remember that Schannel will always negotiate to the highest available protocol. When fully patched, Windows 7/Server 2008 R2 and later Windows operating systems will have at least TLS 1.1 available. Since disabling down-level protocols might cause application incompatibilities, it might be better to use other options to restrict connections to secure systems. Some of these methods, such as firewalls, will be discussed in the later sections of this chapter.

Leveraging network hardware

Network security has long been the task of dedicated hardware devices, and they remain the first and best option to defend computer systems against network-based attacks. Something to remember is that the network is most likely to be a carrier of an attack, not the target for it. It makes sense, then, that the systems used to carry legitimate traffic are involved in the hunt for breach attempts.

Hardware firewalls

Firewalls are quite commonly found at the edge of institutional networks, barricading them against the wild, unregulated environment of the Internet. Many threats will be untargeted searches for targets of opportunity and are easily stopped by even rudimentary firewalls. Most firewalls are focused on stopping unauthorized traffic from getting in. However, many of them can also be configured to selectively prevent outgoing traffic as well. Some attacks that attempt to break into sites try to steal storage space and bandwidth, perhaps to store files for illicit sharing or as a base for a distributed denial-of-service attack. In order to combat this, firewalls can be set to prevent or at least report on any unexpected outbound traffic. This often proves to be more difficult to implement than to discuss. Broad-spectrum blocks usually cause more problems than they solve. However, it is possible to build traffic profiles for individual systems. These can be used to create special rules that are tailored for the IP addresses of internal systems. You can also set a baseline pattern and have triggers set to warn you about inconsistencies.

In addition to external firewalls, some organizations with high security requirements and complex infrastructures might also opt for internal firewalls. For lower security organizations, these can be used to allow more lenient firewalls at the border while using much more restrictive rules for sensitive systems. One benefit of such a separation is that it reduces the strain on the firewalls that are protecting the more secure systems, although this is generally minor. A greater benefit is that network security technicians have less data to sift through and may have an easier time detecting potential compromises.

Firewalls aren't the only specialized network security hardware, although they all operate on the same basic principle: scanning network traffic for threats. Other types of network security hardware might look for other risks, such as viruses, embedded in the payload portions of packets. Some systems watch for evidence of targeted intrusion.

Configuration and maintenance of such specialized hardware usually requires specific expertise. However, the results, typically, are greatly superior to any of those provided by software, especially standardized retail applications. You will need to weigh the costs of such equipment and the personnel to support it against the likely risks that your organization faces, based on the discussion points from *Chapter 1, Introducing Hyper-V Security*. If you're not certain, seek out consulting firms that can analyze your operations and provide recommendations.

Using the virtual switch's isolating technologies

The Hyper-V virtual switch provides a number of features you can use to isolate traffic. Before diving into specific features, we'll discuss its basic switching capability. The virtual switch parses the Ethernet header, just like a typical physical switch. It knows only to deliver frames to the MAC address that they are bound for. This means that one virtual machine isn't going to be able to snoop traffic meant for another port without compromising the Hyper-V configuration.

There are a number of other techniques that Hyper-V's switch uses to enable isolation.

Multiple switch types

Most virtual switches will use an **external** virtual switch. This bonds to a physical network adapter or a team of adapters, and allows direct communication with systems that are external to the guest and its host. Most of this chapter will deal with this type.

However, there are two other modes for the Hyper-V virtual switch: **internal** and **private**. In truth, these modes are nearly identical. The host has a network presence on an internal switch but not on a private switch. The virtual switch can shift between these types by adding or removing virtual adapters for the management operating system. You cannot convert the switch to or from the external type.

The benefit of the internal/private switch mode is that you can be certain that none of its traffic is leaving the host. It is not bound to a physical adapter, and all inter-adapter flow is controlled entirely by Hyper-V. A visualization of the multiple switch configuration is shown in the following image:

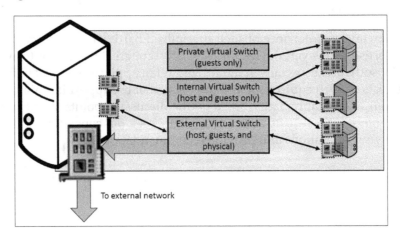

The preceding image shows a host with three virtual switches. As best practice, you should use the least number of virtual switches that can meet your requirements in order to minimize your host's load of network processing.

The primary benefit of the multiple-switch configuration is that it's very easy to maintain and understand. If the intent is to avoid encrypting communications, the overhead of the additional virtual switch is much lower than that of even minimal encryption operations. However, it is not possible for traffic on an internal/private switch to leave the host. So, if the host is clustered, and highly available virtual machines are connected to it, they'll lose the ability to communicate with each other in a migration event. It should also be noted that a change has been made to the management tools in 2012 R2 such that a highly available virtual machine attached to a private or internal switch may refuse to be Live Migrated.

If isolation is the goal, then the loss of connectivity might not matter. You may have a number of guests that you want to isolate from the outside by placing them behind a router, but they have no particular need to talk to each other. To satisfy this, you can use a virtual machine that is running a software router. Give it a presence on an external virtual switch and on a private switch. Connect the virtual machines that need to be isolated to the private virtual switch. Establish an isolated subnet for them and make them use the virtual router. This is shown in the following image:

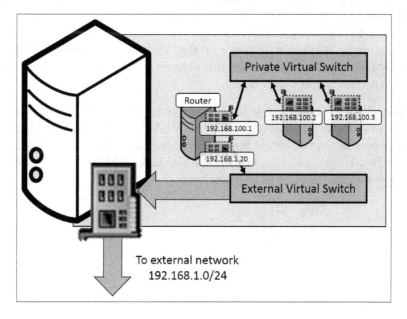

If the isolated virtual machines in the preceding image are highly available, you can place a non-highly available router VM on each host, all using the same internal IP (`192.168.100.1`, as shown in the image). This will allow them to access and be accessible from the external network as desired, no matter which host they connect to, although they'll lose the ability to communicate with any isolated VMs on a different host.

The layout shown in the preceding image is useful if you wish for the virtual machines to have access to the external network. If the virtual machines are running processes that benefit from complete isolation but need access to some sort of service that needs external access, then you can just use a virtual machine with that service instead of the depicted router VM. One such example would be Windows Server Update Services.

Virtual LAN

Internal/private virtual switches are most useful in smaller, less complicated deployments. A more scalable and feature-rich solution is to use **virtual LANs** (**VLAN**). This technology has been a common staple of medium and large networks for a number of years, and is very familiar to network engineers and administrators. A VLAN is a walled-off **layer 2 network**. In a Hyper-V deployment, this means that it will only allow traffic at the Ethernet level to and from those endpoints that are members of the same VLAN. In order for traffic to enter or leave this VLAN, it must utilize a router that has a presence on that VLAN. If you are completely new to this concept, you can read more about it at `http://www.altaro.com/hyper-v/networking-hyper-v-part-2-vlans/`.

What makes VLANs more scalable than the internal/private switch is that virtual machines whose traffic is isolated to a specific VLAN can still communicate with each other even when on different hosts. The only requirement is that all connected physical hardware must be able to recognize 802.1q VLAN tags. The following diagram shows a visualization of this concept:

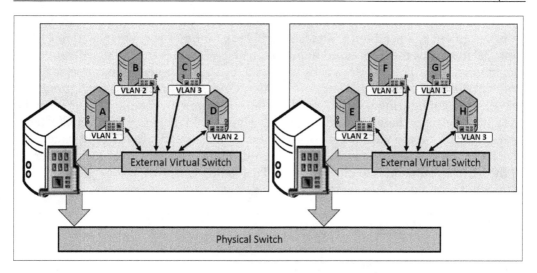

In the preceding image, the virtual machine **A** can communicate directly with the virtual machines **F** and **G** but will need to go through a router in order to talk to any of the other guests. This allows some of the same capabilities of the private/internal virtual switch, in that virtual machines **F** and **G** will be able to communicate with each other using only their host's virtual switch.

> VLANs are layer 2 only, meaning that they only operate at the Ethernet level. Windows machines still require TCP/IP to be configured properly to communicate. Virtual machines in the same VLAN using disparate TCP/IP subnets will still require a router to communicate with each other.

In comparison to the internal/private switch, the drawback of this configuration is that their traffic can and will leave the Hyper-V host. This makes it somewhat more susceptible to being intercepted. The most complicated way this could occur is by a **breakout** (or **VLAN hopping**) attack in which VLAN isolation is overcome. One theoretically possible way to perform such an attack would be to compromise the hardware of a switch. This is extremely difficult under any circumstance and is most probable using known exploits; keeping the network hardware up to date on security patches is your best approach to this issue. The second and much more probable attack method is to set up an unauthorized trunk connection into a switch. This generally requires both physical and administrative access to the network, so following network security best practices is the most effective way to address this risk.

While the breakout risk is very real, it's also extremely difficult. While you should remain vigilant against it, most attackers will look for other ways to overcome your defenses. For medium-sized networks, using VLANs is the preferred network isolation method. The real drawback here, and it's usually a very minor one, is that your network hardware must support VLANs. Once the hardware is configured to use VLANs, configuring a virtual machine for it is extremely simple. On the virtual machine's **Settings** dialog, which is in either Hyper-V Manager or Failover Cluster Manager, click on the virtual network adapter in the left pane. In the right pane, check the box to enable the virtual LAN identification, and then enter the number of the VLAN you want it to participate in. This dialog is shown in the following screenshot with the VLAN set to 2:

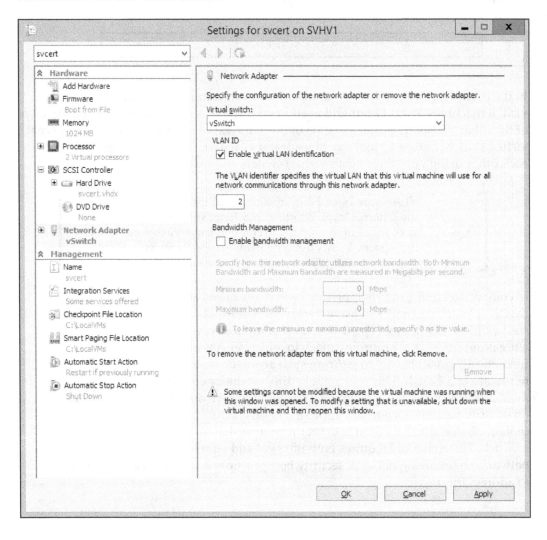

If the management operating system uses only one virtual adapter on a virtual switch, it can be set on the virtual switch's property sheet, also accessible in Hyper-V Manager. However, if it has more than one virtual adapter, such as in a converged fabric design, the only option is to use PowerShell (third-party and/or paid solutions such as System Center Virtual Machine Manager also have the ability to work with them). PowerShell can also be used to set the VLAN for guest adapters.

Using PowerShell to control VLANs on virtual adapters

The three commands that you'll use to operate on virtual adapter VLANs are Get-VMNetworkAdapter, Get-VMNetworkAdapterVlan, and Set-VMNetworkAdapterVlan.

To list all the virtual adapters on a system and their VLANs, just run Get-VMNetworkAdapterVlan without any parameters. A sample output from this command is shown in the following screenshot:

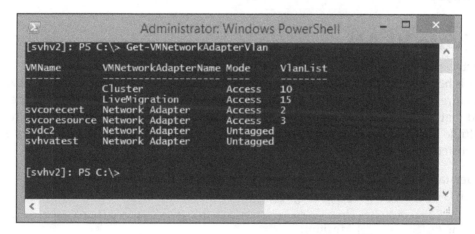

The two adapters in the preceding screenshot that don't list a value for VMName are attached to the management operating system. The rest are assigned to the adapters in the listed virtual machines. These will all be named "Network Adapter" unless you use Rename-VMNetworkAdapter to change them.

Run the following command to change the VLAN for a virtual adapter in the management operating system:

```
Set-VMNetworkAdapterVlan -ManagementOS -VMNetworkAdapterName Cluster
-Access -VlanId 10
```

To clear the VLAN for a virtual adapter in the management operating system, run the following command:

```
Set-VMNetworkAdapterVlan -ManagementOS -VMNetworkAdapterName Cluster
-Untagged
```

To set the VLAN for a virtual machine's adapter, you just drop the `ManagementOS` parameter and use the `VMName` parameter instead. If there's only one adapter, you can even skip using the `VMNetworkAdapterName` parameter:

```
Set-VMNetworkAdapterVlan -VMName "svcorecert" –Untagged
```

If there are multiple adapters in the referenced VM and no name is specified, they'll all be set to the same VLAN.

You can also use the pipeline:

```
Get-VMNetworkAdapter -VMName svcoresource | Set-VMNetworkAdapterVlan
-Untagged
```

Private VLAN

Strictly speaking, a private VLAN isn't about security as much as scalability. This is because much of what it does can be accomplished using the existing VLAN structure. There is a hard limit of 4096 possible VLANs because of the size of the field that holds the 802.1q tag. Private VLANs also enable the same network to host multiple hosts with the same IP address without collisions, which is a good solution for hosted networks.

Understanding private VLANs is mostly a matter of grasping the terminology, which is detailed in the following table:

Term	Meaning
Primary VLAN	This is the same as a standard VLAN.
Secondary VLAN	A secondary VLAN attaches to a single primary VLAN, and through that, its members can connect to the network. The number used to identify a secondary VLAN is not related to any primary VLAN with the same number.
Isolated port	A virtual adapter set as an isolated port cannot talk to the other isolated ports in the same secondary VLAN or any member of any other secondary VLAN. It can communicate with the primary VLAN, which means that it can communicate with other VLANs. It can also communicate with promiscuous ports in the same secondary VLAN.

Term	Meaning
Community port	A virtual adapter set as a community port can communicate with the other community ports and promiscuous ports in the same secondary VLAN and with the primary VLAN, but not with members of other secondary VLANs.
Promiscuous port	A promiscuous port can communicate with all other members of the secondary VLAN(s) it is attached to and with the primary VLAN. The best usage for this type is to connect to a router so it can move traffic for all the other members of its secondary VLAN(s). This is the only type that can be a member of multiple secondary VLANs simultaneously.

In practical terms, if you're not hosting networks for tenants that need isolation or if your network is small enough that the ability to use more than 4096 VLANs isn't appealing, private VLANs are probably more work than they are worth. The requirement for members of a VLAN to communicate through a router to reach other VLANs automatically provides an isolation layer.

If your network can benefit from private VLANs, then your best approach is to work with qualified network administrators to determine what the best configuration should be. While Hyper-V enables private VLANs for its guests, it is not a Hyper-V-specific technology. Improper configuration of secondary VLANs can result in a less secure layout than not using private VLANs at all, so the architecture should be handled by trained network professionals.

Using PowerShell to configure private VLANs

Private VLANs can only be configured using PowerShell, but it's not complicated. All these examples will be applied directly to a virtual machine, which means that if it has more than one adapter, all will use the same settings. You can use any of the techniques shown in the *Using PowerShell to Control VLANs on Virtual Adapters* section of this chapter to select specific adapters.

To set an adapter in the isolated mode, run the following command:

```
Set-VMNetworkAdapterVlan -VMName svisolated -PrimaryVlanId 10
-SecondaryVlanId 15 -Isolated
```

To place an adapter in community mode, use the same structure as the previous command, but replace Isolated with Community.

For the promiscuous adapter, the first change that needs to be made is to use the `Promiscuous` parameter in place of `Isolated` or `Community`. However, because it can be a member of multiple VLANs, you have to use the `SecondaryVlanIdList` parameter instead of `SecondaryVlanId`. This parameter is supplied in the format of a comma-separated list inside quotes, and can use ranges:

```
Set-VMNetworkAdapterVlan -VMName svrouter -PrimaryVlanId 10
-SecondaryVlanIdList "15, 20, 25, 50-100" -Promiscuous
```

If you only need the port to be a member of a single secondary VLAN, the `SecondaryVlanIdList` parameter will accept a lone number.

Network virtualization

The third major method used by the Hyper-V virtual switch to provide isolation is network virtualization. While Hyper-V provides the core infrastructure, you'll need additional plugins to put it to full use. The best option currently available is System Center Virtual Machine Manager. This option will be discussed in *Chapter 7, Hyper-V Security and System Center VMM*.

Employing Hyper-V virtual switch ACLs

The Hyper-V virtual switch doesn't include a full-fledged firewall, but it does have one of the firewall's most important yet basic features. **Access control lists** (ACLs) are simple definitions of traffic rules that allow or deny particular communication types. The basic port ACL was introduced to Hyper-V in the 2012 version, and the extended ACL was part of the 2012 R2 release.

A firewall defines its rules from the perspective of the firewall itself. It controls traffic as it passes through. In contrast, a Hyper-V port ACL is defined directly on virtual adapters and works from their perspective. It's important to remember this as you create ACLs.

The key to the ACL is that it is a list. The most meaningful way to use ACLs is by layering them. This is most commonly done by creating a universal rule that blocks all traffic and then creates exceptions.

Using basic port ACLs

The basic ACL type allows you to control connections between virtual adapters and remote IP addresses or MAC addresses. One possible use for this would be if you had a public-facing web server that uses a SQL server backend. You can use an ACL to ensure that nothing other than the web server can communicate directly with the SQL server. The first thing you need to do is set an ACL that blocks all traffic:

```
Add-VMNetworkAdapterAcl -VMName svsql -Action Deny -Direction Both
-RemoteIPAddress 0.0.0.0/0
```

Next, create the rule that allows traffic to pass to and from the web server:

```
Add-VMNetworkAdapterAcl -VMName svsql -Action Allow -Direction Both
-RemoteIPAddress 192.168.25.210
```

You can continue to add ACLs for other systems, such as update servers, as necessary.

There are a few other options available. Use `Get-Help` to view them. You can choose to restrict access by a MAC address and you can select individual virtual adapters.

Once you've got some ACLs in place, you can view them like this:

```
Get-VMNetworkAdapterAcl -VMName svsql
```

You'll notice that the rules you create with `-Direction Both` will appear as two separate rules: one inbound and one outbound. They can be deleted with `Remove-VMNetworkAdapterAcl`. The rules are not named, so the remove operation will delete all rules that match the parameters that you use with `Remove-VMNetworkAdapterAcl`. In order to perform a granular remove, you'll need to use the pipeline:

```
Get-VMNetworkAdapterAcl -VMName svsql | where { $_.RemoteAddress -eq
"192.168.25.210" } | Remove-VMNetworkAdapterAcl
```

Virtual adapters attached to the management operating system can also be protected by using the `ManagementOS` parameter, often along with `VMNetworkAdapterName`.

Using extended port ACLs

The additional capabilities introduced in 2012 R2 allow you to tune ACLs so that they match specific ports and add the stateful capability. They have the same ability as that of the basic ACL, to block in the IP and MAC addresses, so you can use them to completely replace basic ACLs.

We can use the SQL example from the previous subsection here as well. This time, instead of opening up the SQL server to all possible traffic from the web server, you can lock communications down only to the designated port.

As before, we'll start with a rule that blocks everything. Note the differences from the basic ACL:

```
Add-VMNetworkAdapterExtendedAcl -VMName svdc2 -Action Deny -Direction
Inbound -RemoteIPAddress * -Weight 1
```

The first thing to note is that you cannot specify `Both` for `Direction`. If you need to block or allow traffic in both directions, you'll have to enter two rules. The second thing is that you can use a wildcard for `RemoteIPAddress`.

The third difference is the `Weight` parameter. With basic ACLs, the system simply prioritizes the `Allow` rules ahead of the `Deny` rules. With the additional possibilities granted by the port restrictions, it's possible to have rules that overlap in complicated ways. The `Weight` parameter allows you to precisely control the sorting. Higher numbers take precedence. This is why we set the blanket `Deny` rule to the lowest weight, so that all the `Allow` rules will automatically take precedence.

Next, we can set the SQL rule:

```
Add-VMNetworkAdapterExtendedAcl -VMName svdc2 -Action Allow -Direction
Inbound -RemoteIPAddress 192.168.25.100 -LocalPort 1433 -Protocol TCP
-Stateful $true -Weight 50
```

We've opened incoming connections to the same remote IP address as before, but this time only port 1433, the default Microsoft SQL Server port, is opened for the remote host. We also had to specify the protocol to use; if we also needed to open up UDP, we'd have to create an additional rule.

We've also set this connection to be **stateful**. This means that when inbound traffic triggers this rule, it will watch for outbound traffic that is the inverse. This usually indicates that it is part of the same conversation. If there is an outbound `Deny` rule that would ordinarily block this return communication, it will be temporarily allowed. This means that you won't need to set up a lot of complicated outbound rules in order to have a general `Deny` for outbound traffic.

To remove extended ACLs, use `Remove-VMNetworkAdapterExtendedAcl` in the same way you used `Remove-VMNetworkAdapterAcl` in the previous section.

For further information on these cmdlets, use `Get-Help`. There is also a detailed guide on TechNet, which outlines multiple uses for extended ACLs, at http://technet.microsoft.com/en-us/library/dn375962.aspx.

Practical ACL usage

The benefit to ACLs is that they allow the Hyper-V administrator to control traffic. In an environment in which you have no direct influence over the configuration of the guests, this can help to protect the larger network.

With this power comes a potentially daunting maintenance task. Only rarely will a handful of ACLs completely cover all guests and traffic profiles. If you intend to use ACLs on a regular basis, it's best to pre-create PowerShell scripts that fit particular profiles, such as web servers and SQL servers. Use parameters to set things such as remote IP addresses.

To reduce the effort, it might benefit you to focus on using ACLs on the systems that are at greatest risk, such as those within the perimeter. For others, it will likely be most efficacious to employ a hardware firewall or even the built-in Windows firewall.

Configuring the Windows Firewall

The Windows Firewall is another tool that can be used to protect your systems from network attacks. While you can configure it in the management operating system, this will have no effect on traffic meant for the virtual machines. The Hyper-V virtual switch operates independently of the components that the management operating system's firewall has access to. You can completely block all traffic in and out of the management operating system without impacting the guests in any way.

The Windows Firewall is a common component of all the current Windows servers and desktop operating systems and should be familiar to administrators. As such, we won't be providing detailed instructions in this book. However, there are a number of guides available. Microsoft's TechNet site contains a launching page with a large number of resources devoted to the subject, and is viewable at `http://technet.microsoft.com/en-us/network/bb545423.aspx`.

While the total subject of the Windows Firewall exceeds the scope of this book, there are decidedly fewer resources available on using PowerShell for firewall configuration. In the next section, we'll show examples to help you transition your knowledge of the GUI firewall controls to working with the related PowerShell cmdlets.

Before we move to that section, there are some general best practices to cover:

- Whenever possible, utilize a hardware firewall.
    - Software firewalls are never as effective and they require compute resources. In a dense Hyper-V environment, these computing costs may not be acceptable.

     ° In less demanding environments, software firewalls can be used in conjunction with hardware firewalls to provide defense in depth.

     ° Develop a plan to maintain hardware firewalls. It is critical to stay on top of firewall patches. It's also a good idea to periodically review firewall rules to see if any have become stale or redundant.

- Control firewalls using Group Policy whenever possible. Rules in a central location are easier to monitor and maintain and more difficult for other administrators to bypass.

- Never disable the Windows Firewall service. This often has unintended consequences that break other services without a clear troubleshooting pattern. Instead, if you determine that the Windows Firewall is causing more harm than good, disable the relevant profile.

- Avoid disabling the firewall for anything other than testing purposes. If a program is exhibiting problems when the firewall is enabled, work with the manufacturer to identify the ports that it requires for proper functionality and open them. If that's not possible, there are a number of tools that can show you what protocols and ports are being used so that you can make selective firewall rules. One of these is Microsoft Message Analyzer, which replaced Microsoft's earlier Network Monitor tool. The best place to start with this tool is the related TechNet blog, which contains news as well as links to the download and guides. You can find this blog at `http://blogs.technet.com/b/messageanalyzer/`. Another popular resource is Wireshark, which is freely available at `http://www.wireshark.org`.

- One advantage that the Windows Firewall has over Hyper-V ACLs and hardware firewalls is the ability to assign rules to a particular program instead of just opening a port or protocol. This helps to defend against programs that hijack commonly-open ports. For example, if you have a web server that uses the Apache HTTP server, you can create a firewall rule that only allows port 80 to be accessible to that application. Then, if your web server is compromised by an application that knocks the Apache web server out of commission and sets itself up on port 80, the firewall will not deliver inbound web traffic to it.

Using management tools remotely

We already touched on the topic of running management tools remotely in *Chapter 2, Securing the Host*. To briefly recap, this is the preferred method of remote control. You can use Remote Desktop to connect to the host and run the tools directly, but this requires the host to run a GUI version of Windows Server, consumes a fairly high amount of resources, and presents an interactive session that can be hijacked.

In addition to addressing the weaknesses of Remote Desktop sessions, many remote tools can be configured to manage multiple systems simultaneously. You can even use MMC to design custom consoles that contain the tools that you use most. When used remotely, you'll have a graphic interface even to control Hyper-V Server and Windows Server in the Core mode. However, you'll have to do a bit of work to allow all these tools to connect to your hosts.

Enabling Remote Desktop

Even if using the consoles remotely is usually a better option than Remote Desktop, there is no denying its convenience. Most of the arguments against Remote Desktop are less about security and more about resource consumption, so responsible usage is usually acceptable.

There are a number of ways to enable Remote Desktop connections in Windows. The preferred method is to use Group Policy. Using the instructions provided in *Chapter 3*, *Securing Virtual Machines from the Hypervisor*, in the section *Using Group Policy to control Hyper-V Administrators*, you can use the centralized tool to restrict which users can access the system.

If you must work per system, probably the easiest way is to use the built-in Server Configuration tool. This is a character-mode command line script that runs automatically when you log in to Hyper-V Server, but is available on all varieties of Windows Server. Simply run `sconfig.cmd` in an elevated command prompt, and you'll be greeted with the menu shown in the following screenshot:

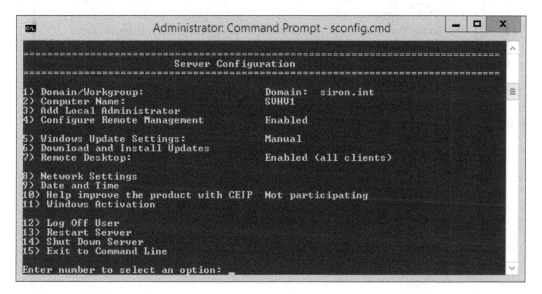

Type 7 and press *Enter* to enable Remote Desktop. First, type E or D to enable or disable the service. If you choose to enable it, you'll then be asked whether you want to allow clients with Network Level Authentication capabilities or all clients that connect. All currently-supported versions of Windows automatically have support for Network Level Authentication, so you should not encounter difficulty with this setting unless you are using non-Microsoft RDP clients.

After you've enabled Remote Desktop, you need to set the firewall. In PowerShell, run the following:

```
Enable-NetFirewallRule -DisplayGroup "Remote Desktop"
```

Be aware that this affects a number of rules. If you want to see all the changed rules, run the following command:

```
Get-NetFirewallRule -DisplayGroup "Remote Desktop"
```

Enabling other remote management tools

The other common tools run inside MMC and use a few common rule groups. Fortunately, PowerShell will work with wildcards, so you can view and manage these groups all at once. To see them, execute the following command:

```
Get-NetFirewallRule -DisplayGroup *remote* | select DisplayName,
DisplayGroup
```

 This command will return the Remote Desktop rules that were shown in the previous section, and for Windows Server only, rules that are part of the Routing and Remote Access module.

You can use normal PowerShell constructs to selectively enable the services that you require. The **Windows Remote Management** group is sufficient for most remote tools to work. You can enable this group like this:

```
Enable-NetFirewallRule -DisplayGroup "Windows Remote Management"
```

You can enable all the remote access groups like this:

```
Get-NetFirewallRule -DisplayGroup *remote* | where { $_.DisplayGroup -ne
"Routing and Remote Access" } | Enable-NetFirewallRule
```

You disable a rule with Disable-NetFirewallRule. The syntax is the same as Enable-NetFirewallRule.

To create your own rule, use `New-NetFirewallRule`. This is a fairly complex command, so you're advised to use `Get-Help` to view all possible options. An example is as follows:

```
New-NetFirewallRule -Name "Custom-Backup-Application" -DisplayName
"Custom Backup Application" -Enabled True -Profile Any -Direction Inbound
-Action Allow -RemoteAddress 192.168.25.207 -Protocol TCP -LocalPort
24251-24252
```

 Starting with 2012, it is not possible to remotely access Device Manager.

Remote access for non-domain-joined machines

Most of these tools require you to use an administrator account. Some also require machine authentication. You may find it necessary to follow the instructions provided in *Chapter 3, Securing Virtual Machines from the Hypervisor* to configure `TrustedHosts` in order for these tools to connect.

Using Hyper-V with IPsec

IPsec is a standard IP security suite controlled by the **Internet Engineering Task Force (IETF)**. Its purpose is to provide network security at the layer of the IP packet. This is a potentially powerful way to secure communications as it maintains end-to-end encryption. It is, however, not a simple technology to implement properly. Encryption at this level can cause problems for the devices that need to deliver those packets. It can also potentially be computationally expensive. You should not be implementing IPsec without an identified requirement and a thorough plan. If you've never worked with IPsec before, there are numerous guides available to help you with the process. Microsoft publishes one such guide that is available at `http://technet.microsoft.com/en-us/library/bb742429.aspx`.

Apart from the potentially high computational burden of running IPsec on a lot of guests in Hyper-V, there's nothing particularly special about running it in a virtual environment. You'll need to configure it inside each guest operating system just as you would in a physical deployment. You can also configure the management operating system to use IPsec, if necessary.

There is one setting that you can use in a Hyper-V setting, and that is to allow IPsec offloading from the guest's virtual adapter to the physical network adapter's specialized processor, if it includes one. This setting can be found on the **Hardware Acceleration** subtab of the virtual adapter's settings in the virtual machine's property sheet, as shown in the following screenshot:

You can also make the change using PowerShell. Instead of using a simple toggle, you can set the number of offloaded security associations. If you use 0, IPsec offloading is disabled. Any other number enables offloading and sets the maximum to the number that you specify. The default is 512. The PowerShell setting is part of Set-VMNetworkAdapter:

```
Set-VMNetworkAdapter -ManagementOs -Name Management
-IPsecOffloadMaximumSecurityAssociation 512
```

Configuring virtual network adapter protections

Hyper-V contains a number of protections that can be applied to virtual adapters. However, these aren't intended to protect the adapter they're applied to, but the rest of the network from specific unauthorized network applications that might be running on the guest that owns the adapter. All of these settings can be found in one location. Open a virtual machine's **Settings** dialog. Expand the virtual adapter you want to work with by clicking on the **+** button to its left. Then, click on the **Advanced Features** subtab. The results appear in the following screenshot, which will be referenced throughout the rest of this section:

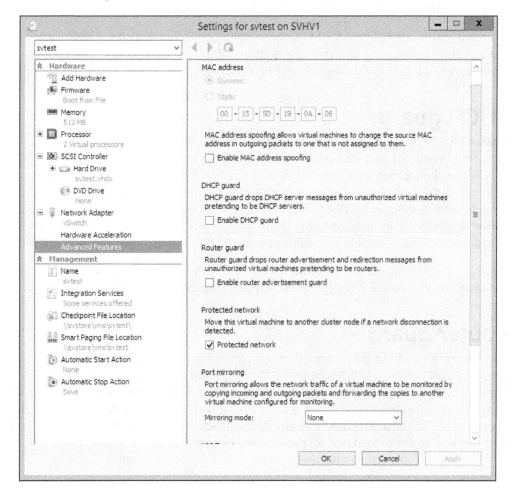

MAC address settings

The initial options we encounter are related to the **media access control** (**MAC**) address of the virtual adapter. This has been traditionally called the physical address as it's usually programmed right into the hardware of physical network cards. It's a networking requirement for all MAC addresses in the same broadcast network to be unique, and for the purposes of safe routing, they should also be universally unique. If one network adapter spoofs or uses the address that belongs to a different adapter, it could impersonate or receive messages intended for that other adapter. Leaving the **Enable MAC address spoofing** box unchecked, which is the default setting, prevents the guest operating system from overriding the MAC address. However, it is always possible for a Hyper-V administrator to override the dynamic address by using the **Static** radio button and entering the desired value.

There are legitimate reasons for MAC spoofing, such as network-load balancers. Unless you're certain that the virtual machine will be providing such a service, it is recommended that you leave this setting disabled.

DHCP guard

When a DHCP client seeks out an IP address for its adapter, it uses specially-formatted broadcast packets on its local Ethernet segment. Checking the **Enable DHCP** guard checkbox prevents the virtual adapter from receiving any of these packets. This means that if a particular virtual machine is running a DHCP server, it won't be able to assign any IP addresses. This prevents the administrator of the guest operating system from inadvertently (or maliciously) circumventing the authorized IP address distribution system. It does not affect DHCP client operations in any way.

There is a very small performance hit involved with this protection, so it's not necessary for you to use it if your guest administrators are trusted.

Router guard

The description field of this setting does a good job in explaining its purpose. Just as a guest operating system might potentially run an unauthorized DHCP server, it could also potentially run routing software. This can allow an attacker to compromise data streams. The risk is a little bit lower than the DHCP issue though, as most TCP/IP endpoints have already been directed to use a particular router and are less likely to try to find one on their own. As with the DHCP guard, there is a minimal impact on performance.

Port mirroring

Port mirroring is not about protecting network endpoints, but it is often used for security purposes. On any given Hyper-V switch, you can designate the **Source** and **Destination** mirror adapters. All frames that cross any adapter marked as **Source** will be duplicated to any adapter marked as **Destination**. In this way, security software can monitor for suspicious traffic activity. Be aware that Hyper-V only provides the frame duplication service; you will need to use software on the destinations ports that can work with it. Such software includes the previously mentioned Microsoft Message Analyzer and Wireshark tools.

Setting Hyper-V protections using Powershell

All the options in this section can be set using PowerShell, which is useful when you want to modify multiple adapters at once. The basic format to change a single adapter is as follows:

```
Set-VMNetworkAdapter -VMName svuntrusted -MacAddressSpoofing On
-DhcpGuard On -RouterGuard On -PortMirroring Source
```

In the preceding command, we've set all the possible options at once, and if the virtual machine has multiple virtual adapters, these settings will apply to all of them. You can use pipelined output from `Get-VMNetworkAdapter` or `Get-VM` to modify multiple virtual machines and/or virtual adapters simultaneously.

Encrypting cluster communications

Computers joined in Microsoft Failover Clusters frequently communicate with each other to ensure that other nodes are active and to send updates on the status of files in shared locations. If a node loses access to a Cluster Shared Volume, it can redirect I/O over another node. All of this traffic is signed by default, but it's also possible to encrypt it.

Using PowerShell, enter the following command to encrypt cluster communications:

```
(Get-Cluster -Name clhv1).SecurityLevel = 2
```

Be aware that this setting can cause increased CPU usage on nodes. Live Migration traffic is not affected nor is any traffic not specifically classified as inter-node cluster traffic. Enter 1 to return to the traffic-signing mode or 0 to turn off both signing and encryption.

Securing Hyper-V Replica traffic

Hyper-V Replica functions by periodically transmitting changes in the live virtual machine's hard disk files to its replica machine over the network. Hyper-V Replica offers three security mechanisms to protect this communication. These are all available from the host's **Replica Configuration** tab. Access it by opening Hyper-V Manager and then right-click on the host and choose **Hyper-V Settings**. The following screenshot will be used as a reference point for the server configuration discussion:

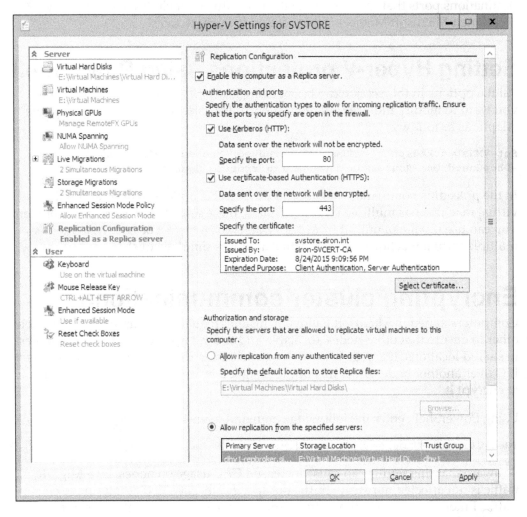

The first group is **Authentication and ports**, where we find our first two options. The first is **Use Kerberos (HTTP)**. When this option is selected, the source host and the replica server will use Kerberos to authenticate each other, but then the replication traffic will move unencrypted. This is the fastest replication option but is the least secure. You should only use it when the connections between the two hosts already have a sufficient level of security. Traffic that crosses an internal LAN is one example. However, you might be transmitting to an offsite location using an encrypted connection, such as a **virtual private network** (**VPN**) tunnel. If this encryption level is sufficient for your requirements, Hyper-V Replica encryption only adds overhead.

If the inter-host network connections are not sufficiently secure, use the second option, **Use certificate-based Authentication (HTTPS)**. This will require you to select a certificate with these options: it must have the **Key Usage** options for the **Digital Signature** and **Key encipherment** options selected; it should also have the **Enhanced Key Usage** setting with the **Client Authentication** and **Server Authentication** options selected, and the key must be marked exportable. This certificate must be assigned to and installed on the Replica host. For cluster members, you must have these certificates for each node, and a certificate must be assigned for the Replica Broker's computer account and installed on all nodes. If you need help with this, refer to the *Configuring the Host SSL Certificate* subsection of the *Leveraging PowerShell Remoting* section of *Chapter 3, Securing Virtual Machines from the Hypervisor*. As with PowerShell Remoting, the source host must trust the certificate authority that issued the Replica host's certificate. If you are installing the certificate, the final option is to restrict from which host(s) the virtual machines are allowed to replicate to this server. By selecting **Allow replication from the specified servers**, you can use the **Add** button to pick the allowed hosts. This opens the following dialog:

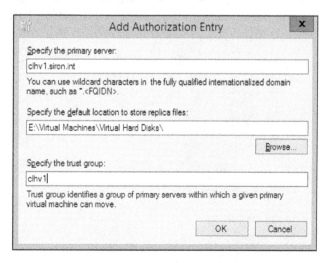

Enter the name of a host or a wildcard match in **Specify a primary server field**. In the second field, enter or browse to the location where virtual machines from this host will be stored if their Replica originates from that host.

The third field specifies which Trust Group you want the host to be a member of. The purpose of this is to control the Replica host's behavior when multiple hosts attempt to replicate the same virtual machine. For example, if a host named HOST1 creates a replica for VM1 and then HOST2 attempts to send updates for VM1, it will only be successful if both HOST1 and HOST2 are in the same Trust Group. Each host can only appear in a single Trust Group.

All of these items can be set using PowerShell. The following lines duplicate the settings shown in the preceding screenshot. Use them as a template along with Get-Help to determine settings for your own system:

```
$CertificateThumbprint = (Get-ChildItem -Path cert:\LocalMachine\My |
where { $_.Subject -match $env:COMPUTERNAME }).ThumbPrint
```

```
Set-VMReplicationServer -ReplicationEnabled $true
-AllowedAuthenticationType CertificateAndKerberos
-ReplicationAllowedFromAnyServer $false -CertificateThumbprint
$CertificateThumbprint
```

```
New-VMReplicationAuthorizationEntry -AllowedPrimaryServer svhv1.siron.int
-TrustGroup clhv1 -ReplicaStorageLocation 'E:\Virtual Machines\Virtual
Hard Disks'
```

You will match the authentication settings when configuring a virtual machine for Replica. Start the wizard by right-clicking on a virtual machine in Hyper-V Manager and clicking on **Enable Replication**, or, if the VM is clustered, by right-clicking on it in **Failover Cluster Manager** and navigating to **Replication | Enable Replication**. Select the authentication parameters on the **Specify Connection Parameters** screen, shown as follows:

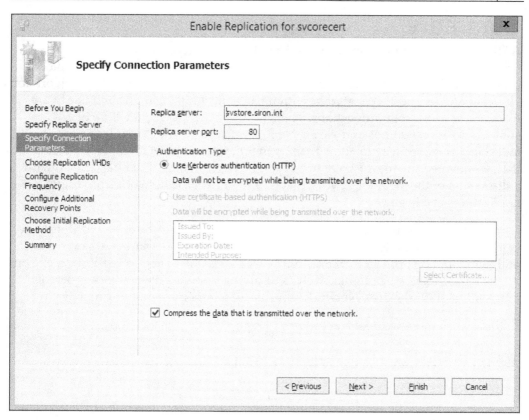

In this example, only **Use Kerberos authentication (HTTP)** is available. This will happen when the target host does not have HTTPS enabled. The opposite will occur if HTTP is not enabled on the Replica host. When HTTPS is selected, you must choose a certificate on the local host (or the Replica Broker's certificate for a clustered guest) that will be used when authenticating against the Replica host.

Summary

As the avenue that most attacks will take in their assault on your systems, the network is the most critical focal point for your security endeavors. This chapter covered the different methods that are at your disposal to lock down the network for Hyper-V and its guests. We started with the benefits of using dedicated hardware to secure network communications. Then, we looked at the Hyper-V virtual switch's isolation features and ACLs. Next, we discussed the Windows Firewall and configuring security to allow management tools to connect remotely. After that, we covered the role of IPsec in a Hyper-V environment. We wrapped up with a discussion of the methods at your disposal to protect the network from rogue applications inside guests.

Remember that this book focuses on Hyper-V. The overall topic of network security is much larger than this or any other single technology. Make sure that you research and follow the best practices. Some things are mandatory, such as keeping an eye on access logs. Others are optional, such as disabling unnecessary network protocols and administrative shares. Network security is an important ongoing activity.

In the next chapter, we'll look at securing Hyper-V's storage locations.

6
Securing Hyper-V Storage

One of the most vulnerable components of your Hyper-V deployment is its storage. If an attacker is able to gain access to the locations that house your virtual hard disks, compromising their data is fairly simple. While most administrators are well aware of the importance of locking down the access points to live storage, many overlook the necessity of using and securing data redundancy systems as well.

In this chapter, we will focus on the following topics:

- Configuring NTFS security for virtual machine storage
- Securing SMB 3.0 shares for virtual machine storage
- Securing iSCSI connections
- Using Secure Boot
- Using BitLocker
- Using Encrypted Cluster Disks
- Understanding the role of backup

Configuring NTFS security for VM storage

Every major component of a virtual machine is stored in a file. Like any file, access must be carefully controlled. If an attacker is able to retrieve a copy of a VM's VHDX file, then it can be easily mounted and its contents can be exploited.

Fortunately, NTFS security for Hyper-V is fairly complete right out of the box. This section is less about what to do and more about what not to do.

Every Hyper-V host has a default location for virtual machine configuration files and a default location for virtual machine hard drive files. Most administrators change these right away for a variety of reasons. This is where we get into our first "don't": don't place virtual machine files directly on the root of an NTFS volume. For one thing, Windows really doesn't want to grant access to files there. For another, modifying security on the volume's root can have serious side effects. Instead, use a subfolder.

Cluster Shared Volumes are attached under the C:\ClusterStorage mount point, so the management operating system does not consider their contents to be in a root. There are no special restrictions against placing items at the top level of a CSV.

When you create a new folder, the following default permissions are assigned:

- The built-in **CREATOR OWNER** object has **Full Control** on all subitems, but no permissions on the folder itself

- The built-in **Administrators** group has **Full Control** on the folder and everything that it contains

- The built-in **Users** group has **Read & Execute** permissions and can create subobjects

- The built-in **SYSTEM** object, which is a security account that represents the computer itself, has **Full Control** over the folder and all contents

There is no need to modify these permissions in any way. What's important is to control membership in the **Administrators** and **Users** groups very closely. You can remove permission to the folder from the **Users** group, but all that this does is add administrative overhead. When the **Users** group's permissions are removed and **User Account Control** is on, you will not even be able to view the security sessions without performing an administrative override.

Once you place a virtual machine in a folder, it is absolutely critical to leave the NTFS permissions alone from that point forward. This is because Hyper-V will automatically assign permissions to subitems as necessary. If anything is changed, particularly with inheritance, this can prevent Hyper-V from being able to even start a virtual machine. The following screenshot shows the permissions assigned to a virtual machine's VHDX file:

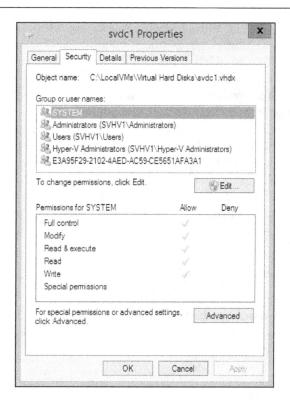

The first three items are inherited from the parent, which are the defaults. When the virtual machine was created, Hyper-V set permissions for Hyper-V Administrators and the virtual machine itself. The last item that you see is the GUID that represents the virtual machine that this virtual hard disk is attached to. If this permission is lost for some reason, the virtual machine won't turn on. The fix is relatively simple: use Hyper-V Manager or PowerShell to detach the virtual hard disk and then re-attach it. However, the preventive measure is to just leave NTFS permissions alone. Rather than controlling the access control lists, control membership in the existing groups.

In some situations, the special Virtual Machines account, which we were introduced to in the Group Policy section at the start of this chapter, will appear in NTFS security lists as well. If you place virtual machines on a Cluster Shared Volume, Hyper-V will grant that account a number of permissions on the automatically-created subfolders. If its permissions are removed, they can be difficult to replace as the account does not show up in any of security lists. This means that you can't just use Windows Explorer to add the account's permissions in. If you need to repair a folder that's had its permissions damaged, the quickest thing to do is reset all the permissions at the highest level folder that hasn't been broken so that the system has full control, and then enable inheritance and import the virtual machine into Hyper-V. It will automatically reset the permissions. If this doesn't work or isn't an acceptable approach, you can use the built-in tools to create another VM in another location. That folder will have the necessary security settings. You can then duplicate them in the folder that lost the settings with the following:

```
Get-Acl 'C:\ClusterStorage\GoodVM\Virtual Hard Disks' | Set-Acl 'C:\ClusterStorage\BrokenVM\Virtual Hard Disks'
```

If you wish to simply re-assign the permissions, use the following script (modified from a script previously published at http://www.altaro.com/hyper-v/free-script-fixing-hyper-v-folder-security/):

```
$FolderToFix = Get-Item 'C:\ClusterStorage\BrokenVM\Virtual Hard Disks'

$SIDToFix = Get-Acl $FolderToFix

$SIDToFix.SetSecurityDescriptorSddlForm($SIDToFix.Sddl + "(A;;0x12008f;;;S-1-5-83-0)(A;CIIO;DCLCGR;;;S-1-5-83-0)")

Set-Acl $FolderToFix -AclObject $SIDToFix
```

The script may fail if the account which you're logged in to doesn't have the necessary permissions. The best thing to do is use an account that has permissions. If this is not an option, then you can use the following command line (not PowerShell):

```
Takeown.exe /f C:\ClusterStorage\BrokenVM /a /r /d y
```

This command will change ownership of the indicated folder and all the subitems to the local Administrators group. You can run `takeown.exe /?` to see all options.

Again, the best option is to take preventive measures by not modifying NTFS permissions.

Securing SMB 3.0 shares for VM storage

A very closely related topic to NTFS permissions is the securing of SMB shares. While the permission model for shares is much simpler than that of NTFS, it follows the same basic pattern.

There are a growing number of commercial devices that can expose SMB 3.0 shares. They may have some of their own needs. If you own or are planning to own one of these devices, make sure that you work with the manufacturer to properly configure any necessary security settings to satisfy your organizational requirements.

If your SMB 3.0 share is running on a Windows Server 2012 R2 system, remember to disable CIFS/SMB 1.0. We showed you how to do that in *Chapter 2, Securing the Host*, but it's worth repeating:

```
Remove-WindowsFeature -Name FS-SMB1
```

Next, lock down the share itself. Unlike NTFS permissions, Hyper-V will not get involved with the configuration of a share.

> Remember that NTFS and Share permissions are cumulative. Each of these is first determined separately, and then the more restrictive of the two is applied to connections that come through a share point. NTFS is more granular than Share permissions and are always applied, so it is recommended that you exert maximum effort to ensure that NTFS permissions are correct and then set **Share restrictions** permissively enough for connections to work.

As with NTFS permissions, there are default permissions. In this case, the only thing that happens is that the **Everyone** group is given the **Read** permission. This time, we'll want to make changes. These are the recommendations:

1. Remove the **Everyone** group
2. Add the local **Administrators** group with **Full Control**
3. Add the local **Hyper-V Administrators** group with **Change**
4. Add the computer accounts of any systems that will need to operate virtual machines on the share with **Full Control**

Fortunately, **Share** permissions aren't nearly as difficult as NTFS permissions to change in PowerShell, starting with 2012:

```
Revoke-SmbShareAccess -Name VMs -AccountName Everyone

Grant-SmbShareAccess -Name VMs -AccountName Administrators, SVHV1$,
SVHV2$ -AccessRight Full

Grant-SmbShareAccess -Name VMs -AccountName 'Hyper-V Administrators'
-AccessRight Change
```

Notice that the cmdlet is intelligent; even though we didn't specify that some of the accounts were local and others were from the domain, it is able to automatically locate them.

If you are creating an all-new share, the settings are even easier, and you can set the folder ACL as well (if the folder already has running virtual machines, only add the share and its permissions; do not run `Set-SmbPathAcl`):

```
$NewFolder = New-Item 'D:\VirtualMachines' -ItemType Directory

New-SmbShare -Name VMs -Path $NewFolder.FullName -CachingMode None
-FullAccess Administrators, SVHV1$, SVHV2$ -ChangeAccess 'Hyper-V
Administrators'

Set-SmbPathAcl -Name VMs
```

As you're setting the Share permissions right at the creation point of the share, it's not necessary to explicitly exclude the **Everyone** group. The function of the last line of that script isn't obvious; it sets the NTFS permissions of the folder that hosts the VM's share to be identical to its Share permissions. This can have a destructive effect if the folder's permissions are already set and it holds virtual machines.

You can view all the shares on a computer with `Get-SmbShare`.

The SMB 3 specification also includes the ability to encrypt its traffic. For a Microsoft system, you can set this while creating a share in Server Manager. It's also a parameter on both `New-SmbShare` and `Set-SmbShare`:

```
Set-SmbShare -Name VMs -EncryptData $true
```

That's all that's necessary for encryption of SMB 3 shares in Windows. However, SMB 3 devices might need something more.

Administrative and hidden shares

All Windows operating systems contain a number of default hidden shares, commonly known as **administrative shares**. These are locked down only to members of the local administrators group, backup operators, and the built-in **INTERACTIVE** account. They do provide an access window for extremely sensitive areas of the system. As with the advice given here, the best thing to do is to ensure that you control membership in the relevant security groups, because modifying these shares can have unintended consequences. If desired, you can also remove these administrative shares, although some return automatically on reboot. They're not greatly useful for a Hyper-V host, but remember that some things, such as backup software, may be dependent upon them. Since these have no more value on a Hyper-V system than any other, you can operate on them the same way you would on a standard Windows Server.

These shares are created by default and are also hidden. This means that when a remote computer browses it, they won't appear. They do show up on the local system when running `Get-SmbShare` or `net share`. The share can only be accessed by entering its full name completely. A hidden share is distinguished from a standard share only by a dollar symbol at the end of its name. The access control rules work in the same way.

You can work with them in the same way you work with any shares, that is by using Windows Explorer or the PowerShell cmdlets from the previous section. You can learn more about the administrative shares from this Microsoft knowledge base entry at `http://support2.microsoft.com/kb/314984`.

Securing iSCSI connections

Naturally, iSCSI travels across the network. In their natural form, the packets are easy to decode. If they're intercepted, an attacker will have no problem in extracting their contents. Unless steps are taken, an attacker can also pretend to be a host with legitimate access to the iSCSI target, and read its contents that way. There are a few ways to protect them.

Physical and logical isolation

The best way to protect iSCSI traffic is to put it on physical network hardware that has nothing in common with anything else. With that precaution taken, there's usually nothing else necessary to lock down iSCSI communications. This has an additional benefit of lowering the amount of network traffic that iSCSI traffic needs to contend with. Due to the way that switching works, this is usually insignificant unless there are many hops.

The following diagram shows one architectural option to isolate iSCSI:

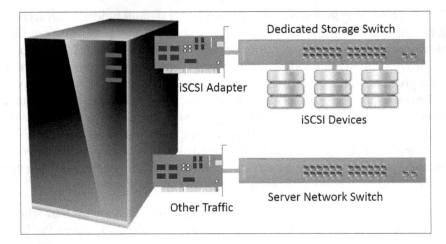

Another option is to use logical isolation. You can employ a common switching fabric but use VLANs without routing capabilities to achieve security that is similar to that in the preceding diagram. An attacker can compromise this by using the techniques discussed in the VLAN section of *Chapter 5, Securing the Network*, so it's not quite as secure. It does use less hardware and is easier to maintain.

iSCSI security options

If iSCSI traffic must cross common networks, or if the basic security discussed in the previous section is not sufficient, there are a number of options available to directly secure it. Configuration of these options on the target (the system or device where the storage resides) will depend on the manufacturer's design, and you'll need to consult their documentation to configure that side. However, all these settings need to be configured on the initiator side as well, so we can discuss each of the available options from the perspective of the built-in Microsoft iSCSI initiator.

 If the manufacturer of your target device also provides special initiator software, it's recommended to use that.

The graphical interface for the iSCSI initiator can be opened in any edition of Windows, even if it's not a GUI edition. Simply run iscsicpl.exe. In GUI versions, you can also access it by opening the **iSCSI Initiator** item under **Administrative Tools**.

This book does not intend to teach you the basics of making iSCSI connections. You can review Microsoft's documentation at `http://technet.microsoft.com/en-us/library/ee338480(v=WS.10).aspx`. What we want to focus on here is security.

Remember that there are two components in a connection to an iSCSI target: the portal and the actual target. These two entities can be secured separately. This is often necessary as you might use a single portal to cover multiple targets that have different security requirements. Within the Microsoft initiator, the settings dialogs for both look the same. We will use the **Advanced Settings** dialog box to connect to a target as the basis that we'll work on. A screenshot of the first page of this dialog is as follows:

The first thing that we will discuss from the preceding screenshot is the **CRC |
Checksum** section. These are more about data integrity than data security, although
they could potentially catch packets that have been tampered with. They both work
the same way, but on different parts of the packet. Like all other TCP/IP packets,
an iSCSI packet is composed of a header segment and a data segment. The header
contains enough information to clearly delineate the proper sender and receiver. If
this is modified by an outside source but the checksum isn't, then the change can be
detected. Likewise, the data can be protected. It must be reinforced that these are
not truly intended as security measures. Modifying the checksum isn't more difficult
than modifying the header or data to begin with. These settings also incur a minor
performance penalty, with the header digest being less expensive. Settings on the
initiator and the target must match, or communications will be rejected.

The second portion is about the **challenge-handshake authentication protocol**
(**CHAP**). Unlike checksums, CHAP is designed for security. However, it does not
protect data. It verifies that one or both participants in a conversation are who
they say they are. The section shown in the preceding screenshot is only about
configuring information for the target. The entry in the **Name** field is what this
initiator will present to the target for logon authentication. Changing this usually
involves more administrative overhead than what can be justified by any potential
security enhancements. The better option is to use a complex and well-protected
entry for **Target secret**. This is a shared secret, so it must be set exactly the same
way on the target.

The next setting on this dialog is **Perform mutual authentication**. When not selected,
the initiator will use the information you entered in the previous two fields to
authenticate to the target, but it will not verify the target's identity to check whether
it is correct. If you do select this, it will perform reverse authentication against the
target. You'll need to configure the secret that it expects from the target, but that's
in another location. We'll return to that later.

The last two checkboxes are for the **Remote Authentication Dial-In User Service**
(**RADIUS**) authentication. Instead of presenting credentials to each other, the
initiator and/or the target will use a central authentication server that must be
configured separately. These checkboxes enable the RADIUS authentication for
the specific portal or target. You configure the RADIUS server information on the
RADIUS tab of the initiator's dialog. This is an easily understood screen and won't
be explained here.

Remember that CHAP does not encrypt or protect the data. All it does is help to ensure that the initiator and, optionally, the target, are not impersonators. For true data protection, you must use IPsec. This is provided by IPsec, which is configured on the next tab on the **Advanced Settings** dialog for IPsec, as shown in the following screenshot:

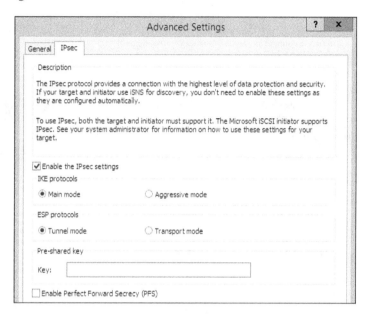

There aren't many items to set here, but we will cover a bit of the terminology. **Internet Key Exchange (IKE)** is how the initiator and target authenticate with each other. Aggressive mode is less secure, but faster. **Encapsulating Security Payload (ESP)** is the technology that encrypts the data. The difference between tunnel and transport mode is that the tunnel mode encrypts the original IP header and adds another for a tunneling midpoint. The network will carry the packet to that tunneling device, which will retrieve the encrypted IP header and send the packet to that destination. Some devices operate in tunnel mode, so both headers might be the same.

The next item on this tab is the **Pre-shared key**. As with all such keys, it must be the same on the initiator and the target.

The final item is **Enable Perfect Forward Secrecy (PFS)**. When set, the systems will use multiple public keys to communicate with each other. This means that any one packet captured won't be useful in comparison with another to determine the private key.

The global iSCSI settings are where we'll find the remaining security components that we previously mentioned. They can be found on the **Configuration** tab of the main iSCSI dialog. This dialog and page are shown as follows:

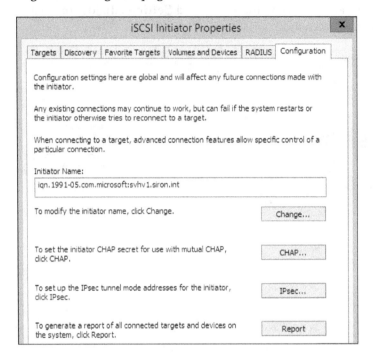

The buttons we want to focus on are **CHAP...** and **IPsec....**. We'll start with the CHAP dialog, as it's the simplest. It only has a single field, and that is for **Initiator CHAP Secret**. If this system connects to a target and enables reverse authentication (by checking the **Perform mutual authentication** checkbox on its **Advanced Settings** dialog, as explained earlier), then that target must present this secret for the initiator to allow the connection.

The **IPsec** button opens a dialog where you can add entries to an internally maintained list of target IPs behind IPsec tunnel gateways. The **Destination Address** field is for the target while the **Outer mode address** field represents the tunnel gateway. If the target is operating in tunnel mode, then both IPs are the same. If necessary, you can also restrict the connection to the designated target to a specific adapter and the initiator IP by using the respective drop-down boxes.

A few iSCSI settings can be controlled by Group Policy. Most of the settings only restrict the ability of local administrators to connect to remote targets. They cannot be used to define targets. Access these settings at **Computer Configuration | Administrative Templates | System | iSCSI**.

Using Secure Boot

The aging **basic input/output system** (**BIOS**) that has controlled PC-based systems since the beginning is gradually being replaced by a new system known as **Unified Extensible Firmware Interface** (**UEFI**). Most of the differences have little to do with security and instead address technological shortcomings of the earlier system. The big security difference is in **Secure Boot**. Hyper-V brings this to its guests in Generation 2 virtual machines, introduced in 2012 R2.

In Hyper-V, Secure Boot defends against malicious software taking over the boot process of a virtual machine's operating system. It maintains a database of signatures for trusted operating systems. If any guest operating system doesn't match an entry in the database, then Hyper-V won't allow the guest to boot. Windows 8 and 8.1 desktop operating systems and Windows Server 2012 and 2012 R2 server operating systems will boot inside a Generation 2 virtual machine configured for Secure Boot; other operating systems will not. If you're using a known good operating system that refuses to boot because of a Secure Boot error, first verify that there's no non-OS bootable media attached to the system. If there isn't, then something has happened to the guest operating system, and it should be treated as compromised.

To set Secure Boot in PowerShell, execute the following command:

```
Set-VMFirmware -VMName svgen2 -EnableSecureBoot On
```

To reverse the setting, use Off instead of On. You can set it in the GUI in the virtual machine's dialog box on the **Firmware** tab. There is a checkbox titled **Enable Secure Boot**. This setting can only be changed while the virtual machine is off.

Using BitLocker

One of the biggest problems in computer security, especially storage, is physical security. If someone is able to take a hard drive, it's usually not difficult to overcome most security barriers to access its data. BitLocker is a solution to this problem. It provides whole disk encryption and secure boot (which is different from UEFI Secure Boot). In order to gain the most out of BitLocker, it should be used only from the management operating system and on a computer with a **Trusted Platform Module**. BitLocker is a standard Windows component and won't be discussed in depth in this book. For more information, start with Microsoft's documentation at http://technet.microsoft.com/en-us/library/hh831713.aspx.

BitLocker will have the most value in any installation where the physical safety of a computer cannot be guaranteed and the physical storage has no other protective mechanism. BitLocker has its drawbacks though. Drive encryption always incurs performance overhead, sometimes substantial. It's also problematic in the event of hardware failure. Since the purpose of BitLocker is to prevent a hard drive from running on any machine other than the one it was initially enabled on, it won't start if you need to transplant the drive even for legitimate reasons. The best cure for this is to take regular backups.

BitLocker protection can also be extended to cluster disks, including Cluster Shared Volumes. The complete procedure is detailed on the Clustering and High Availability blog at `http://blogs.msdn.com/b/clustering/archive/2012/07/20/10332169.aspx`.

Understanding the role of backup

Security has two meanings. Throughout this book, we've focused almost exclusively on the definition that involves defending systems from malicious attacks. There's also a more generic definition that, in our context, just means keeping data and systems safe. For most installations, the most probable risks don't come from attackers. They come from accidents and system failures. The only meaningful defense you have against these risks are good and regular backups. As a side benefit, backups can also help you to recover from attacks that damage your data. Quite simply, backups are not something that any organization of any size can afford to be without.

Unfortunately, backups present a risk of their own. Numerous data breaches have occurred through theft of unencrypted backup tapes. No matter how well the live data is protected, it's meaningless if the backup data isn't equally well protected.

The first recommendation is to use encryption. Since backups aren't live, performance is much less important. This means you can use higher-strength encryption protocols with relative impunity. The second thing to consider is transport and storage security. It's a standard best practice to keep backups in a location other than the primary site to protect against disaster scenarios. It's vital that any physical transport be handled by trusted personnel and that the offsite location be securable within reasonable needs of the organization.

One way to cover a number of these bases is to use a cloud-based backup solution and provider. Most of these providers encrypt the data both in transit and on their own storage. It's offsite, so it protects you against disasters.

Whatever method you choose, in keeping with the more general definition of "security", it's important that you regularly perform test restores of your backed-up data. This is not only to partially ensure that any disaster recovery scenarios you have designed will operate as intended, but also because backup operations sometimes fail, and backup storage media is often not as reliable as live storage media.

While we haven't discussed Hyper-V Replica in this book, the same principles that apply to a replica infrastructure apply to a backup scenario as well.

Summary

This chapter was focused on the considerations for storage security and the techniques at your disposal to address them. We started off by discussing NTFS and SMB security. Next, we looked at ways to protect and secure iSCSI connections. After that, we discussed the benefits of Secure Boot and BitLocker. We wrapped up the chapter with a discussion on backup.

In the next chapter, we'll move from looking at Hyper-V alone and take up the subject of System Center Virtual Machine Manager and its role in protecting your virtual environment's infrastructure.

7
Hyper-V Security and System Center VMM

So far, we've covered a number of different security concepts, both from a guest VM's perspective and from the perspective of the virtualization host itself. These concepts apply to standalone Hyper-V hosts and Hyper-V failover clusters alike, but what happens when **System Center Virtual Machine Manager (SCVMM)** is thrown in the mix?

In some perspectives, SCVMM (sometimes simply referred to as VMM for short) makes our lives as system administrators easier as it is an enterprise grade tool that commands our entire virtual infrastructure and backend fabric. Some will say that this makes the configuration of security concepts and best practices easier, but at the same time, we're adding complexity to the mix. Added complexity means we have a potentially larger attack surface that we need to cover from a security perspective.

While SCVMM itself doesn't really change the Hyper-V security playing field a whole lot, it does bring some interesting concepts to the table. This includes things like role-based groups for VM and fabric administration, multi-tenant virtualized network separation, and the Windows Azure Pack.

Each of these items provide their own perks and benefits, but we need to leverage them in a way that is effective from a security perspective and in a way that is easy to manage.

The other thing to note about SCVMM and the features mentioned here is that they are designed with the goal of managing multiple on-premise private clouds in a way that allows complete separation of data and network traffic if needed. These are some of the concepts we'll be covering in this chapter.

This chapter will briefly cover a few security-conscious sections of the SCVMM installation. If additional information is needed, it can be found at `http://technet.microsoft.com/en-us/library/gg610617.aspx`.

In this chapter, we will focus on:

- Enhancing Hyper-V host security through VMM
- Securing the VMM installation itself
- Network virtualization and multi-tenancy
- Providing secure self-service with the Windows Azure Pack

Enhancing Hyper-V host security through VMM

In the world of management tools, it's highly important that the base-level functions of the underlying product are generally left intact. That said, SCVMM does a really good job of building on top of the existing functionality of Hyper-V and failover clustering. It provides additional functionality on top of an already strong feature set. This is very much the way SCVMM is in the realm of system security as well.

VMM, for the most part, relies on the underlying Hyper-V security concepts that have been discussed in chapters 1 to 6 to do the heavy lifting, but one thing that VMM really helps with, though, is more secure management of Hyper-V hosts.

Prior to SCVMM, being in play, we didn't really have a whole lot of granular control over who has access to what functions and features. Really, it came down to who was in the local Hyper-V administrator's group and who wasn't, which isn't all that helpful in certain situations.

What happens when you need to provide "very" granular access to particular functions? For example, a level 1 help desk technician needs to be able to control the power state of virtual machines in your virtual infrastructure. We can facilitate this easily through some of the role-based groups that are present inside of VMM.

To get a feel for the role-based groups that are present in VMM, you can dig around in the **User Roles** section of VMM, located under **Settings** | **Security** | **User Roles**.

While you can use this area of VMM to create custom role groups, it should be noted that there is a built-in administrators' group inside of VMM that is out of the box, if that is enough to suit your needs.

Once here, you can click on **Create User Role** on the action bar at the top of the SCVMM console. You'll be greeted with the wizard as follows:

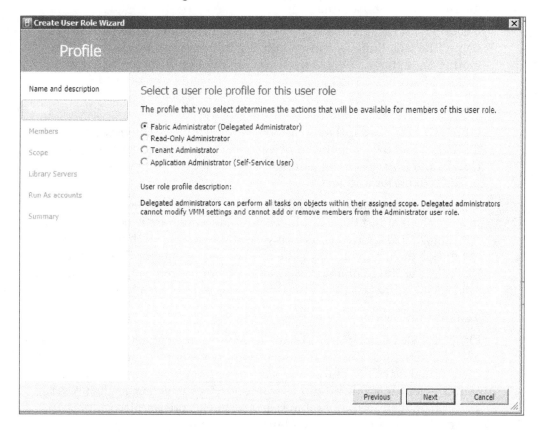

Here, you can see a number of predefined role groups that you can use to define a custom role inside of your VMM instance. Each role group has a predefined list of what it can do. You, as the VMM admin, can tailor this list to suit your individual needs.

The user role group descriptions

Let's review what each predefined role group is:

- **Fabric administrator (delegated administrator):**

  Official VMM description: Delegated administrators can perform all tasks on objects within their assigned scope. Delegated administrators cannot modify VMM settings and cannot add or remove members from the Administrator user role.

  Basically, this role group can do pretty much anything within the target scope. The only thing that users utilizing this predefined role can't do is modify the settings of VMM itself and modify user membership of the Administrator user role.

- **Read-only administrator:**

  Official VMM description: Read-only administrators can view properties, the status, and the job status of objects within their assigned host groups, clouds, and library servers, but they cannot modify the objects. This user role is suitable for auditors.

  This role is exactly how it sounds: read-only. This can be extremely useful in several situations though. Maybe your infrastructure is being audited. Auditors like to see that you're only assigning the rights that are needed to get the job done, so you may get some brownie points for that. In addition, this role is useful to monitor users and software. You need to keep tabs on your virtual infrastructure. This role is designed for such tasks.

- **Tenant administrator:**

  Official VMM description: Tenant administrators manage self-service users and VM networks. Tenant administrators create, deploy, and manage their own virtual machines and services by using the VMM console or a web portal. A tenant administrator user role specifies which tasks the users can perform on their virtual machines and services, and can place quotas on computing resources and virtual machines.

  This user role is highly useful in situations where you may want to delegate control of a certain department's VMs, users, and services to someone within that group. This lessens the administrative burden off you and provides the end user with access to only the items that are utilized by their department. This is also applicable for service providers in providing VMM access to a customer that may have resources attached to this VMM instance.

- **Application administrator (self-service user)**:

  Official VMM description: Self-service users create, deploy, and manage their own virtual machines and services by using the VMM console or a web portal. A self-service user role specifies which tasks the users can perform on their virtual machines and services and can place quotas on computing resources and virtual machines.

  Think of this one as a narrower and more specific subset of the tenant administrator user role in that the self-service user role cannot manage other self-service users and VM networks. Self-service users are also manageable by tenant administrators.

 You'll see this information again in *Chapter 8, Secure Hybrid Cloud Management through App Controller*, in a much more abbreviated form as this info is important and highly relevant to security discussions around both SCVMM and App Controller, which is covered there.

These four groups really form the building blocks for the role-based management and security that SCVMM and System Center App Controller provide. Additionally, you can use any of these four groups to make even more specific groups if needed. Let's continue through **Create User Role Wizard** and its review. Please have a look at the following screenshot:

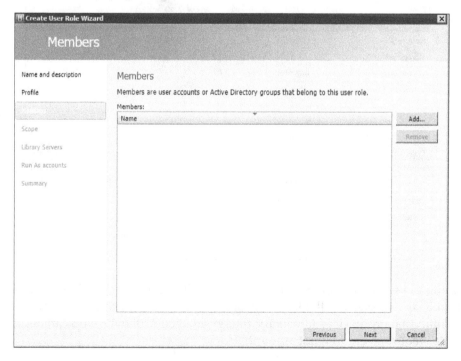

The next screen allows you to attach some AD-based user accounts into our new SCVMM role group. This can be done with either individual user accounts or entire groups. This allows you to leverage your existing AD infrastructure to start carving up who can do what inside VMM.

If you are building a private cloud to provide services to external customers or entities, it is **strongly** recommended that you build an entirely separate AD infrastructure from that of your internal directory services. This ensures separation from external users that are not part of your organization and provides increased security.

After adding the users and groups that you want into the wizard, you'll then be asked to define a **scope**. The scope is a group of target resources that this user role will be managing. This is how you keep the HR tenant administrator from doing anything with the sales department's virtual infrastructure. This is the level of granularity you want when it comes to limiting access to certain pieces of your environment. Additionally, depending on the role group you selected, you may be asked to define resource quotas for the said group, as follows:

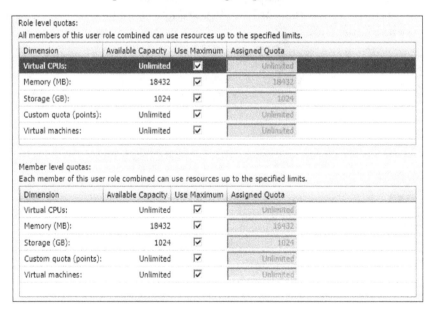

One thing to keep in mind when defining quotas is that the top section is for this group role as a whole, and the lower section defines the quotas for each individual user within that group. This allows for fine-grained control over who can deploy compute resources and to what amount.

The next screen will define what virtual networks the role is allowed to utilize. This will tie in, somewhat, with the multi-tenancy discussion later in this chapter, followed by the resources section of the wizard, which will allow you to get even more granular with regard to scope targeting. You can pick individual VMs and services in this section of the wizard if needed.

Additionally, you'll be able to set what library share the members of this particular group can use to gain access to VHDs, ISO, and so on, as follows:

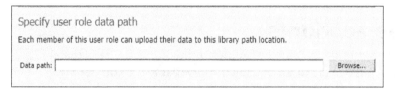

Then, finally, once we reach the permissions section of the wizard, we can see the meat and potatoes of the user role. This is where the true granularity of SCVMM user role groups lie.

As you can see in the following image, we can define exactly what a user can and can't do to the resources that were defined earlier in the wizard. This includes things such as limiting the creation of checkpoints or only allowing the group to start and stop VMs as we mentioned in the L1 help desk technician example earlier.

Another thing to note in this section of the wizard is that you can define these settings globally across all resources that were selected or just a portion of them. Please have a look at the following screenshot:

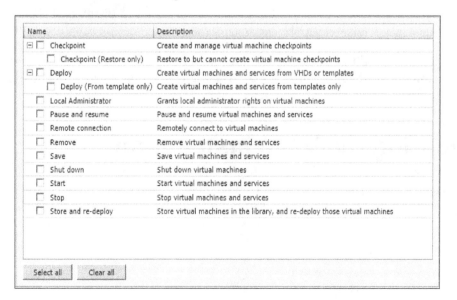

After finishing with this section of the wizard, you'll be given a summary of the settings for your newly created group. Click on **Finish** and you're good to go! You've just created an SCVMM-based role group.

From a host security perspective, placing limitations on user accounts reduces the risks associated with a compromised account, and prevents users from messing with things they aren't supposed to be messing with. They will only see what they are scoped out to see. This goes a long way towards securing your hypervisors.

Run as accounts

The other benefit that SCVMM provides in this same arena is the ability to create **Run As Accounts**. This can be reached in the same section of the VMM console: **Settings | Security | Run As Accounts**.

Think of **Run As Accounts** as saved credentials but saved in such a way that end users cannot see what the credentials actually are. This allows us to do some really cool things as far as host management is concerned, because now, we can save a set of credentials that would allow a normally restricted user to perform a particular task with the elevated permissions stored in **Run As Account**.

The other nice thing about this feature is that VMM does a pretty good job of notifying you when needed. A good example is when connecting a VMware ESXi cluster to VMM. The credentials for the target vCenter server get stored in **Run As Account** for use at a later time as needed.

Another thing to note about this feature is that the run-as accounts themselves should follow the rule of least access. The reason behind this recommendation is that when a standard user utilizes the run-as account, they are using it with the full rights and powers associated with that account for the targeted task. With that in mind, it is not recommended to put the domain admin in place as a run-as account. Instead, it is recommended that you make compartmentalized accounts with just the needed rights to complete the target function.

Securing the VMM installation

We've talked about what SCVMM brings to the table as far as assisting us in securing our host environment is concerned, but what about VMM itself? How do we keep VMM secure? Once in place, VMM is intended to be the overarching management tool for your entire virtual infrastructure, so it's critical that it is secured at all times.

Well, the good news is that VMM does a pretty good job on its own of being a fairly secure service. It mostly leverages all the underlying technologies and techniques that have been covered in this book up until this point. However, it still doesn't hurt to say that it's extremely important to ensure that all the standard security best practices are followed. This includes keeping patches up-to-date and limiting who has access to what via the role-based administration features, but what else?

There are a couple of key pieces during the installation of SCVMM that should be noted, which we'll quickly cover here.

 As mentioned earlier, this chapter will only be covering the security-specific sections of the installer; thus, if you are installing a new VMM instance, keep an eye out for the following sections as they do have some relevance to the security of your VMM installation.

The first section of the installer that we'll review is the **Database configuration** section of the installer (shown in the following screenshot). While the fields here are quite self-explanatory, there are some considerations to be made.

It is recommended that you define an account in your AD infrastructure to act as the service account for VMM. This allows you to narrow down the rights for the VMM user account to just what is needed to run VMM. This includes the needed rights to the SQL instance and associated DB, and while we could lock down these permissions at a later time, the best practice is to be secure right from the point of installation, so we'll cover this now. Please have a look at the following screenshot:

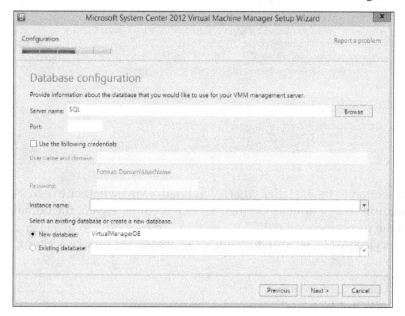

With this in mind, the service account that has been created in AD for VMM should be given the following SQL permissions to make it least permissive at the time of this writing:

- The domain account should be added into SQL as a new login

- The allowed configured server roles for the account should be `dbcreator`, `process admin`, and `security admin`

- The user should be mapped to the target VMM DB and configured with the `db_owner` role membership

The next section of the installer has a couple more fields that warrant some consideration:

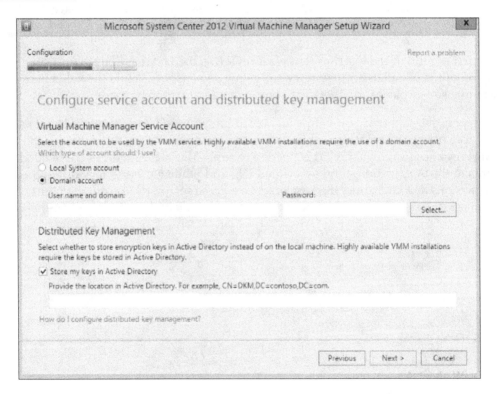

This is the section of the installer where you'll tell VMM whether to run as **Local System account** or as a domain-defined service account. Again, the domain service account is the recommended path. This setting can be modified at a later date by using the services MMC snap-in to modify the associated service account.

Additionally, on this screen, you'll see the section for distributed key management. While you could have the encryption keys stored locally on the machine, it is highly recommended that you store them in AD, as AD is designed and security hardened to store this type of information when utilized correctly.

These are the encryption keys for VMM's communications and internal functions. You want to take extra care that the container inside AD that holds this information is configured with very restrictive user rights. Most of the following permissions should be in place by default, but it's best to check after installation to verify that unwanted permissions aren't propagated down the directory tree for some reason.

Verify that the target container contains the following permission settings:

Entity	Rights	Target
System	Full control	Container object
Administrator	Full control	Container object and all descendent objects
Domain admins	Full control	Container object and all descendent objects
Enterprise admins	Full control	Container object and all descendent objects
Enterprise domain controllers	Read token groups	Descendent user, group, and computer objects
Your AD VMM service account	Full control	Container objects and all descendent objects

The next screen in the wizard will allow you to modify the ports that VMM uses for communication. While it is usually recommended that you go with the defaults, some security-conscious organizations may find it beneficial to modify these settings. However, if you do indeed go that route, make sure all of the associated firewall rules are updated accordingly. Otherwise, you'll have problematic communication issues that may be difficult to track down without revisiting this wizard.

With these items configured properly from the get-go, VMM can be quite secure and difficult to breach due to its inherent ties to the active directory.

VMM library shares

Another section of VMM that some folks tend to forget about is the VMM library share. This function is quite often a set-it-and-forget-it type of thing, but as it is a part of VMM, it makes sense to cover it briefly here.

The general rule of thumb for the VMM library shares is that your administrative user accounts will require read/write access to the library shares that are used to store general-use ISOs, VHDs, and so on. All other users will have read-only access to these shares so they can use the associated resources to deploy VMs and services. The other option in this space is the ability to carve out library shares for self-service users and provide read/write access to them. This allows you to provide a department head, or external customer with the ability to create and upload their own resources into their library share for use at a later time, without allowing people outside of that scope to see those same resources. This is all controlled via your normal NTFS file and share permissions.

Anything else?

Another thing to verify is that you have all the needed firewall rules for VMM in place and configured properly. The full list can be found at the TechNet link as follows:

```
http://technet.microsoft.com/en-us/library/gg710871.aspx
```

Network virtualization and multi-tenancy

So far, we've talked about several hypothetical situations where you may have multiple segregated departments or external customers deploying and managing multiple resources inside of SCVMM. We've covered separating out individual access to resources using role groups, and from a compute perspective, the virtualization layer does a very good job of isolating virtual workloads from VM to VM, but what about virtual networking? If these entities are all utilizing the same hypervisors, all virtual machine guest traffic is most likely going out across shared links, right? How does VMM help us separate out that traffic?

Historically, this has been a function that has been taken care of by creating dedicated VLANs for each individual entity. VLANs are still a viable option in today's world. However, the utilization of VLANs can become problematic when scaled out beyond a certain point, and it requires quite a bit of management from some sort of network operations team to set up and maintain those VLANs across an enterprise-sized network. Additionally, in an age where businesses are looking to do more with less, you may not have all the needed network operations man power you need, so the more we can put in the hands of the virtualization administrator, the better.

How does Hyper-V and the Microsoft virtualization stack assist with this problem? The Hyper-V Extensible Switch has the bells and whistles to tackle this problem through its network virtualization capabilities. These capabilities can provide complete customer/department network segregation on the same LAN segment, even if two entities have similar IP addressing schemes.

When we say "like IP addressing schemes" we don't just mean similar. Two servers that contain the exact same IP address could communicate over the same physical LAN segment and not have issues, even without VLANs.

This is all made possible by the logic built into the network virtualization stack that is present in Hyper-V and SCVMM. The next question you're going to be asking is "How does this not cause network issues?". This is a valid question, as under normal circumstances this would cause IP address conflicts, and traffic simply wouldn't flow correctly.

Hyper-V and SCVMM approach this problem by assigning two different IP addresses to the virtual machine. On one side you have the customer or tenant address, which is the address that your customer or department is accustomed to seeing, and on the other side, you have what is called the provider address. This is the address that your private cloud infrastructure sees at the hardware layer to do the normal packet routing and transmission. The following diagram shows customer traffic:

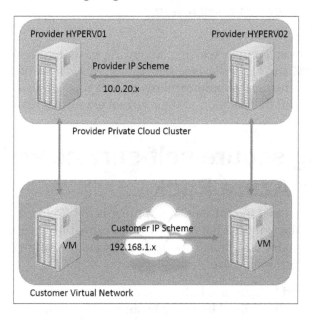

As shown in the previous image, customer traffic is allowed to traverse the virtualized network normally and is unable to talk to the physical network using that same IP scheme. When it attempts to do this, the network virtualization protocol that is built into the Microsoft virtualization stack will use the provider IP addressing schemes for any hardware-to-hardware packet transfers, or when a customer's VM has to traverse the physical network to talk to a VM on another host.

At the packet level, this approach is achieved by encapsulating the packets from a customer's virtual machine inside another packet that contains the relevant provider's IP information. This allows each individual Hyper-V host to route packets to the appropriate destination based on the information in the packet and a separately-defined virtual subnet contained within VMM that is created when boarding the tenant.

Even based on this brief description, it's not hard to see how this simplifies the separation of customers/tenants at the networking layer. This allows us to run multiple workloads from multiple sources on the same private cloud infrastructure while maintaining the security of isolation of one tenant from another.

Without a doubt, this topic could fill several chapters of a book, and it is the purpose of this book to instruct on the security needs and implications of Hyper-V and SCVMM and **not** the complete setup and configuration of individual features within the product set. That said, an excellent guide for implementing this technology is available at `https://gallery.technet.microsoft.com/Hybrid-Cloud-with-NVGRE-aa6e1e9a`.

This guide will get you on your way in configuring the network virtualization features of SCVMM and Hyper-V. Needless to say, this is possibly one of VMM's most powerful features, and should certainly be looked at by anyone who is looking to further separate out the isolation of their virtual environments.

Providing secure self-service with the Windows Azure Pack

It's no longer a secret that the future of computing is the cloud. Several large-scale corporations have thrown their hats in the ring in providing a public consumable cloud computing model, and there is perhaps no cloud computing platform as revolutionary as Microsoft Azure.

Microsoft has poured billions and billions of dollars into building out a global public cloud infrastructure that is used by many businesses today as the backbone of their enterprises. However, not all use cases merit the use of a public cloud platform. Maybe you have some strict industry regulations that require all computing resources and data to stay on-premise, or maybe your CEO is just plain scared of those stormy-looking clouds. Whatever the reason, what if you could leverage some of the enhancements designed for Microsoft's public cloud in your own on-premise private cloud? Would you do it?

One such enhancement that is available is the Windows Azure Pack. The Azure Pack is the same UI that is presented to Microsoft Azure users. This interface can be presented and pushed down on top of an internal SCVMM installation to provide the same experience as the use of the public Microsoft cloud.

Now, you may ask, what does this have to do with Hyper-V security? Well, as the world of mobile computing becomes more and more the norm in our industry, you will, at some point, need to manage your SCVMM instance remotely. This can be done via a number of different methods: RDP, App Controller (discussed in the next chapter), and so on. The Windows Azure Pack provides a full feature-management approach for nearly all the functions within your private cloud.

Once again, we won't be covering the installation and architecture of the mentioned production in detail. As this book is focused on security, some best practices with regard to securing the Azure Pack will be covered. If you need more information on the architecture and installation of the Azure Pack, refer to `http://technet.microsoft.com/en-us/library/dn296432.aspx`.

The nice thing about the Azure Pack is that it's a modern web-based utility. Because it's a web-based utility, we can guard it from threats, much like we would protect any other hosted website from attacks. We use a combination of things such as IP filtering, DOS attack prevention, frequently-changed credentials, and so on.

The simplest and easiest form of securing your Windows Azure Pack portal is frequently-changed passwords. If you haven't changed the password to your admin portal in several months, do yourself a favor and go do that after reading this chapter. Hardened credentials are your first line of defense. In addition to the password, security-conscious organizations may want to think about changing the username on a regular basis as well, because an attack can't attempt a brute force for a username it doesn't know. This is something to keep in mind.

On top of frequent changes, the credentials for each website role should be unique to mitigate the risk if one of the said accounts end up being compromised.

This can be done by performing the following steps:

1. Log in to the management portal.
2. Select **Web Site Clouds** and then select the applicable cloud.
3. Under the **Credentials** and **User Name** sections, edit and update the password for each listed website's role.

Following this concept will harden your Azure Pack infrastructure in the event that you are compromised somehow, and will make it more difficult for an attacker to cause damage to your organization.

In addition to credential management, IP filtering should be configured on the management portal so that only trusted IPs can reach it. This will include IPs from entities such as branch sites or remote employees. I will even go so far as to say that remote employees are required to access the Azure Pack management UI over a VPN connection; this way, you don't have to account for the rapidly-changing IPs of the modern day consumer ISP market. If an administrator connects in with a trusted VPN connection, they'll likely be on some sort of internal IP address that can easily be trusted within the Azure Pack configuration.

This can be configured in the **Web Site Clouds** section of the management portal under **Block List**. A single IP or an entire range can be defined here, so there is plenty of flexibility.

If you're more the Windows PowerShell type, IP filtering can be configured by utilizing the following commands in order:

```
Add-PSSnapin WebHostingSnapin

Set-HostingConfiguration -WorkerRegKeyRejectPrivateAddresses 1

Set-HostingConfiguration -WorkerRegKeyPrivateAddressRange <Beginning of
range>, <End of range>
```

Once this is done, you need to restart the Dynamic WAS Service, which can be completed by running the following commands at an elevated command prompt:

```
net stop dwassvc

net start dwassvc
```

DOS and DDOS attacks

Moving on, another type of attack that can be difficult to protect web-based applications from is a DOS style attack. DOS attacks are particularly malicious in that they siphon all the resources from the server, and in doing so, prevent all meaningful use of its functions. This is accomplished by flooding the target server with so many requests that the system is unable to keep up, which results in the consumption of all available resources.

A high security firewall should be able to help mitigate the risks involved in this type of attack. However, if you don't have a firewall with such features, the next best way of guarding against this style of attack is by setting quotas on the various resources associated with the app. This includes CPU, memory, bandwidth, and storage. The idea is that when the quota for any of these resources is reached (and it will be reached during a DOS attack), the website will go offline, which hopefully may dissuade any further attacks from this source, and give you some time to bolster your defenses prior to bringing the site back online in the event that the attack continues.

While we're talking about DOS attacks, it may be worth mentioning that as the Azure Pack is a web app, it's best to follow all of the best practices with regard to network firewalling concepts. Only NAT and port-forward the ports and services that absolutely need it. Also, when applicable, set up a DMZ that is separate from your production's network. This provides an additional layer of complexity that an attack has to navigate in order to get to the goods.

Following these best practices will allow you to harden your Azure Pack installation against future attacks and provide consistent access to the great tool that the Azure Pack is with regard to the management of your on-premise private cloud.

Summary

In this chapter, we discussed at length what SCVMM brings to the table with regard to Hyper-V host/guest security. We also reviewed how network virtualization and some of the new features of the Hyper-V Extensible Switch allow us to fully separate out multi-tenant environments across the same physical network fabric. This includes identical subnets across tenants. Finally, we discussed the use of the Windows Azure Pack for management of on-premise private clouds and the best practices involved in hardening that utility against attacks.

In the next chapter, we'll discuss System Center App Controller, which, like the Azure Pack, sits on top of SCVMM to provide enhanced management capabilities. Many of the same basic security concepts for web applications discussed in *Chapter 7, Hyper-V Security and System Center VMM*, can also be applied to *Chapter 8, Secure Hybrid Cloud Management through App Controller* and can also App Controller, so keep this in mind as you read on.

8
Secure Hybrid Cloud Management through App Controller

The previous chapters primarily focused on securing our hypervisors, VMs, networks, and storage. *Chapter 7, Hyper-V Security and System Center VMM* introduced and explained what System Center Virtual Machine Manager brings to the table in the realm of on-premise private cloud management. However, we are yet to talk about the tools that are available to securely manage multiple clouds at once.

As organizations and businesses increasingly move to Microsoft's new "Cloud OS" strategy, managing multiple resources in multiple locations is going to become a challenge. Doing this in a secure manner is going to be much more of a challenge.

So, what tools are available to help us tackle this issue? We need to be able to securely manage on-premise SCVMM installations, but we may have resources elsewhere as well. What happens when we need to manage resources inside an Azure public cloud subscription? What if we need to manage resources contained within a service provider datacenter? How do we securely manage those resources?

Sure, we could use the respective SCVMM clients and the Microsoft Azure management portal, but this certainly doesn't make management simple or cost effective. Time equals money, and the quicker that IT pros can get the job done, the happier the management is and we can conduct our efforts as system administrators more securely.

Additionally, what if we could provide delegated access to managed cloud resources in a way that is simple and role-based with the ability for them to be accessed from anywhere via an easy-to-use web interface? You'd go for it, wouldn't you?

The tool that really fits the job in this situation is a little known System Center add-on called App Controller. What you'll find as you read through this chapter is that App Controller really simplifies security when managing multiple clouds. As you're providing a single unified interface to allow your IT staff to administrate several clouds, you have one portal to secure and facilitate. Simply put, the less tools that are in play, the less things there are to be compromised by an attacker.

Let's review what App Controller can do, and see how it can help us manage public and private clouds in a secure fashion.

In this chapter, we will focus on the following:

- System requirements for App Controller
- Installing App Controller
- Connecting clouds to App Controller
- App Controller's role-based security model

System requirements

Before we can plan for or install any new application, we need to know what the requirements for the said application are. App Controller doesn't need much, but there are some things that administrators need to be aware of prior to installation.

One thing that isn't readily apparent before the installation is that App Controller is really an addition to a pre-existing System Center Virtual Machine Manager instance; thus, if you don't have this present inside your environment and you're looking for this functionality, go get your house in order first. App Controller doesn't have to be installed on the same server as VMM, but the VMM server must be specified during the installation process and thus be reachable by the machine that will be running App Controller.

In addition, for App Controller to be leveraged properly, all of your various fabric resources inside of VMM need to be configured, and at least one Cloud has to be defined inside of VMM. Again, your house needs to be in order.

A SQL instance will also need to be defined since App Controller relies on SQL for its database backend. For small deployments, you may be able to run this DB on the same server that is hosting App Controller. This may even be the same server that is running VMM if your App Controller deployment is a POC in a lab, but it is recommended that you define a remote instance of SQL for larger deployments and install App Controller on its own server, separate from VMM.

Additionally, the following are the system requirements:

- Pentium 4 and a 2 GHz (x64) minimum CPU with dual-core 2.8 GHz (x64) recommended
- 1 GB RAM minimum with 4 GB recommended
- 512 MB free disk space with 1 GB recommended
- Supported OS and SQL versions as defined by TechNet at `http://technet.microsoft.com/library/dn249764.aspx`
- .NET Framework 4.5 and WCF data services
- Microsoft Web Services (IIS)
- The VMM console must be installed on the machine that is hosting App Controller

 If .NET and IIS are not installed prior to launching the App Controller installation wizard, the installer will install the required packages to fill those two requirements automatically.

Also, please make note of the following performance and scale limitations as mentioned by TechNet at the time of this writing (`http://technet.microsoft.com/en-us/library/dn249764.aspx`):

- 900 objects allowed in a Windows Azure storage directory
- 5 VMM management servers connected at once
- 20 Azure subscriptions allowed per user
- 75 concurrent users
- 10,000 maximum jobs that can be run in a 24 hour period

Most people will not run into these limitations, but it's wise to know what they are, should the need arise. None of us usually plan on scaling that large, but always plan for the unexpected.

With regard to client-side system requirements, you only need to have a web browser that is Silverlight 5-capable, such as one of the more recent versions of Internet Explorer, but as we are talking about managing our environments in a secure manner, it is highly recommended that you procure the latest supported version of IE for client-side management.

Now that we've covered the requirements, let's move onto installation, as there are a couple of security considerations to take into account during the installation process.

Installing App Controller

The first thing that you need to do is procure the software and the product key from Microsoft. Make sure that you grab the latest version as well. If you're like most administrators, you'll probably see multiple versions available in the Microsoft licensing portal.

 This chapter discusses and demonstrates App Controller being installed in an on-premise location. It is possible to host and run App Controller directly from an Azure subscription, but certain requirements have to be kept in mind. For more information on this deployment method, please see the SC: App Controller System Requirements page on the TechNet website (`http://technet.microsoft.com/library/dn249764.aspx`).

Once you have the software and your product key, you can mount the ISO (or extract the files) and proceed with the installation. Let's look at it step by step:

1. Launch `Setup.exe` to bring up the intro screen. You'll notice that the **Use Microsoft Update to check for updates to App Controller setup** option is checked by default. I see no reason for anyone to ignore this option, so please leave it checked. Microsoft found bugs and/or security issues in the setup that they deemed worth fixing.

2. Simply click on **Install** to continue the process.

3. At this point, you'll be prompted for your product key. If you opt to not insert the key at this time, App Controller will be installed in the evaluation mode. Insert your key (or don't), and click on **Next**.

4. Accept the license agreement and click on **Next**.

5. At this point, the installer will check to see whether the VMM console, .NET, WCF Data Services, and IIS are all present. The VMM console will have to be installed manually if it isn't present. The others, however, will be installed automatically as part of the installation process. Click on **Next** to continue.

6. Select the installation path next. It's usually recommended to stick with the default installation path of `C:\Program Files`.

    This is the point where we start to have some security considerations during the installation. You'll see in the following screenshot that we can tell the App Controller service to run as either **Domain account** or **Network Service account**:

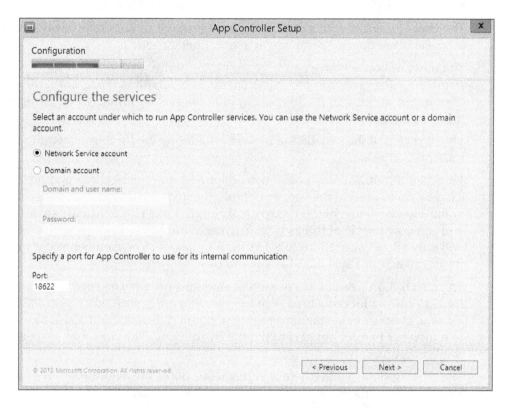

The Network Service account will have minimum privileges on the local machine and is presented to the network as the computer itself. This is all well and fine, and is used quite often as the account running the App Controller service, but there may be times when adding in strictly-controlled file shares to App Controller may require some additional file permission changes. This is one downside to using a Network Service Account. Just something to keep in mind!

Our other option here is to define a domain account to be used to run the App Controller service. A domain service account can be both a blessing and a curse. They are much easier to manage as they plug right into your directory infrastructure, but you can shoot yourself in the foot from a security perspective if you aren't careful. A domain account should be created *specifically* for this purpose, and should be locked down in all other regards (for example, interactive logins disabled, and so on).

The benefit you get with a domain account is that it can be easier to allocate access to other domain resources at a later time if needed.

The other option we have on this screen is the ability to define a port number for the service to communicate on. The default is 18622, but it can be customized as needed. As this port is quite unique, it's unlikely that changing it will be necessary.

The next step of the installation process will define the IIS-related settings for App Controller.

There are a couple of key points here, the first being the bindings and port used by IIS to present the site. By default, the installer will accept connections to the site via all unassigned adapters through port 443. To increase security, you can do a couple of things here. You can modify the bindings so that IIS will only allow connections to a specific adapter/IP. You can then route that traffic out across a specific VLAN if you have to.

The next option would be to use a non-standard port. It's no small fact that hackers know a lot of secured web services that are presented on port 443. You can choose a non-standard port here if you'd like, but you'd also have to remember to force-connect to the site by utilizing that same port as well, so plan accordingly.

The other option we have here is perhaps one of the most important. We can sign the web traffic to and from App Controller with an SSL certificate. You can either have it generate its own certificate or utilize one from a third party, such as Verisign or GoDaddy. It is highly recommended that you utilize a third-party certificate authority as it adds another layer of security on top of your installation and makes it more difficult for your defenses to be breached.

If this is a production installation, don't mess around with this. Just go get a third-party certificate. You'll thank yourself in the end. Take a look at the following screenshot:

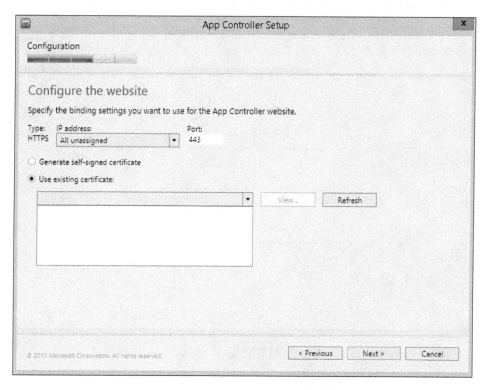

7. The next step of the installation will ask for SQL Server details. Enter the server name, SQL instance, and the port for connectivity to the target SQL instance.

8. At this stage, you pretty much have to click on **Go** and the installer will take care of the rest!

Voila, you now have a production-ready App Controller instance (assuming everything with the installation was successful). By default, you can access the App Controller interface via a Silverlight-enabled web browser via the address `https://serverhostname/`.

Next, we'll be covering how to connect App Controller to all those private and public clouds that we want to manage.

Connecting clouds to App Controller

On connecting to your new App Controller interface, you'll be greeted with a screen that looks similar to the following screenshot:

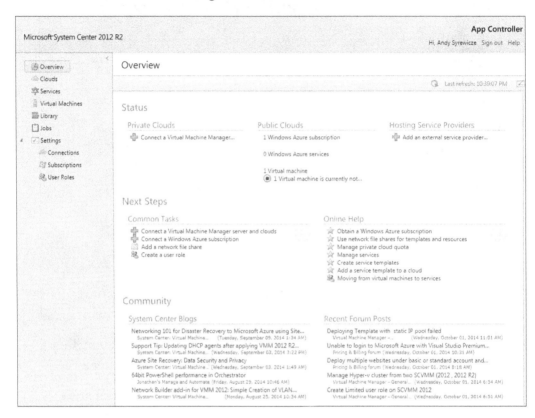

One difference you may notice is that in the preceding screenshot, an Azure subscription has already been added to App Controller. We'll cover that shortly.

 As App Controller attaches itself to an existing VMM instance, any user that is a member of the VMM Admin's group will be able to log in and connect all the various resources to App Controller.

To begin the process of adding all of your various public and private clouds to App Controller for management, you simply have to click on one of the corresponding links. As one of the most common usage scenarios for App Controller is to delegate secure web access to VMM resources to an internal department, let's start by adding in our local VMM instance under the **Private Clouds** section. Click on **Connect a Virtual Machine Manager...** to start the wizard. Take a look at the following screenshot:

You'll be greeted by the screen shown earlier and you'll have to walk through the following steps:

1. You'll start by giving your connection a meaningful name, because once you start adding more clouds into this portal, you want each name to be very self-explanatory in order to avoid confusion.

2. Next, give the connection a description.

3. In the **Server name** field, you'll enter the FQDN of the target VMM server and the port used to connect to the said VMM server. The default is port 8100 and should be changed to match your VMM server if you modified that port setting during the VMM server installation. It's an extra hassle, but could be a viable increased-security option for high-security organizations. The fact is that attackers know the standard ports used for various services. If you're changing things, it keeps them guessing.

4. Finally, you'll see that the **Automatically import SSL certificates** option is selected. This will automatically import the necessary certificates into the App Controller DB to allow secure file and template transfers to and from the VMM instance. If you're planning on using this functionally, then you want to leave that selected. If left unchecked, you simply won't be able to move those resources in and out of the said VMM instance.

At this point, App Controller will connect to the targeted VMM instance, pull down any applicable SSL certificates, and pull in the associated inventory objects that might already be present inside VMM.

Congratulations! You can now manage your on-premise private cloud via App Controller's simple (and powerful) web interface.

However, in order to copy and move files and templates via the web interface, we have an additional step to do. We need to add in a network file share to App Controller.

This can be done by clicking on the library section on the left-hand column and performing the following steps:

1. Select **Shares** from the middle column.

2. Click on **Add**.

3. Enter the share path and click on **OK**.

This can be the VMM library share where you store your VM templates and ISOs, or it can be any other share that you want App Controller to have access to.

One thing to note though is that any share that you plan on accessing with App Controller will need to have an entry added to the security permissions at the folder level. All App Controller server computer accounts will need to be given **Full Control** access to the shared folder in question.

Now, as this is just the computer account and not a full-blown user account, this isn't much of a security concern, but some organizations may require stricter security than that, so you might have to choose between ease of use or security, which is often the case when we're talking about IT security considerations.

Once the share is added, you'll see it populated in the shares section in the middle column, and you're now effectively managing a VMM instance or private cloud through the App Controller interface.

The next most-likely step in the configuration of App Controller is to add either an Azure subscription to the interface for management or connect to a service provider cloud. The configuration steps needed to connect to both are very similar in that during the Azure connection wizard, you enter the Azure subscription ID you'd like to connect to, and in the service provider cloud connection wizard, you enter the "service location" information.

In the grand scheme of things, you're essentially telling App Controller to do the same thing. Connect to a remote entity and manage it securely over firewall-friendly port numbers such as port 443.

A couple of other things happen in the background, such as certificate handshakes and checks to verify that the App Controller instance is allowed to manage the target cloud.

As the industry is seeing widespread adoption of Azure, we'll cover the steps needed to connect securely to an Azure subscription, after which you'll be able to practically follow the same steps to get connected to a service provider cloud. Let's walk through it step by step.

The first thing we need to do is create a management certificate. This can be done via an Enterprise PKI (Public Key Infrastructure) if you have this infrastructure in place. If not, it's not that difficult to install the Active Directory Certificate Services role and get it configured to the point to where it can serve this function.

Regardless of what certificate you use, there is one recommendation that you must keep in mind. Whatever certificate you choose, use it solely for this purpose. Stop and think about it for a second. You're going to tell Azure to allow a connection from App Controller and allow it to do anything it says. You want this traffic to be secure, and though it is difficult enough to break the encryption on an SSL certificate, if the certificate is not shared and used elsewhere, it's less likely to be targeted. This is something to consider.

Once you've determined where the certificate is coming from, you need to have access to both the .cer file for the certificate and the .pfx file as well. The .cer piece of the certificate will get uploaded in the target Azure subscription, which we'll cover now:

1. Log in to the Azure management portal for the target subscription and click on the **subscription** link in the top right-hand corner.

2. Select **Manage Subscriptions | Directory**.

3. Make a note of the Azure subscription ID on this screen (we'll use it later) and click on the **Management Certificates** tab near the top of the screen.

 This screen contains a list of all the associated management certificates that tie into the specified Azure subscription. If you've not set up any ties in Azure previously for the target subscription, you might not see anything defined on this screen.

4. Select the .cer file that is associated with the management certificate and click on the check mark to upload the file to Azure.

5. Click on the **Connect a Windows Azure Subscription** link on the App Controller dashboard. At this point, you will see several fields that need to be configured. We'll step through each, one at a time.

6. Name the connection. Again, meaningful names are a helpful reminder to you as the administrator. Anyone else managing the environment will appreciate it as well.

7. Add a description for the connection.

8. Copy in the Azure subscription ID that you found in step 3.

9. Click on **Browse** and select the .pfx file associated with the management certificate, then enter the password for the file in the bottom field.

10. Click on **OK**. If all is well, the subscription will now show as connected on the App Controller dashboard, and any resources contained within the subscription should start to populate in the view.

The preceding screenshot shows all the required information needed to connect App Controller to an Azure subscription.

At this point, App Controller is now managing both our internal private clouds and any public Azure clouds that we might have.

In this event, there is a service provider cloud that you would like to connect to; the process for doing this is pretty much the same. You'll need the service provider's supplied certificate information and the service provider's management URL in place of the Azure subscription ID and your self-supplied certificate.

At this point, App Controller is connected to the clouds needed, and we can begin to use it to manage our environments.

App Controller's role-based security model

As this book's primary focus is on Hyper-V security, we're not going to spend much time actually discussing the use of App Controller in connecting to VMs, installing services, and so on. Those who are curious will find that App Controller really looks and feels like System Center VMM itself, so the actual use of App Controller you'll find is very intuitive; however, let's move on to some more security-focused talk.

Now that we're connected to our target clouds and are managing our environment through App Controller, let's take a moment and talk about App Controller's role-based security model.

If you remember, earlier in the chapter, we had to define a VMM server for App Controller to tie in to. App Controller has a number of inherent benefits with regard to security because of this, such as the following:

- App Controller uses the underlying security model and user roles that are defined inside the target VMM instance.

- App Controller has ties with Active Directory as well. This is due to the fact that App Controller pulls its security from VMM, which draws its user/group security from AD, providing central management for the users that will ultimately get assigned into a role-based group inside VMM and App Controller.

- App Controller will not allow a user of any level to view or manage the fabric resources of the VMM instance. This provides simplified administration for those users that have fabric resource access, and provides an additional layer of security in keeping those users who do not have fabric access away from those resources and settings.

 As stated, App Controller prevents all users from accessing fabric resources. This is by design as it's assumed that all underlying infrastructure is ready and configured prior to deploying App Controller. If fabric resources need to be managed, this can be done via the SCVMM Console as always.

Again, due to the fact that App Controller has close ties with VMM, all of its role-based security is built on top of what is defined in VMM. In order to see the necessary groups inside of App Controller, they must first be defined in VMM under **Settings** | **Security** | **User Roles**.

When we create a user role, we're really saying that the defined user role is allowed to do X, Y, and Z to resources A, B, and C. This could be operations as granular as only allowing a user to see certain clouds or only be able to start and stop VMs. However, all user roles will fall somewhere within the four available user role profiles. Think of these as the building blocks for our defined security roles. Let's review each of them:

- **Fabric Administrator (Delegated Administrator)**: Think of this as your superuser role. It can perform all functions on all targeted objects.

- **Read-Only Administrator**: This role is really intended for monitoring purposes. It can read the attributes and settings of a targeted resource, but is unable to modify anything.

- **Tenant Administrator**: Users in this role have somewhat elevated rights. Users assigned to this role can manage things, such as self-service users, VMs, service deployment, and more. Review the role permissions screen inside VMM to see the full list.

- **Application Administrator (self-service user)**: This role is intended for individuals and end users. Assigned users can conduct operations on resources deployed by them.

App Controller's role-based groups will ultimately be based on one of the four role profiles mentioned, and the said groups can be granularly managed in VMM with regard to the specific allowed functions of each profile.

With regard to the delegated management of Azure subscriptions, this can be done at a role-based level as well as via the **Settings | User Roles** section of the App Controller interface. You can define a new group that consists of any number of AD users/groups, and then define the scope by selecting the applicable Azure subscription you would want the users to have access to. You'll also have the option to define those users as "read only," which will only allow them to review the existing workloads in the defined Azure subscription and not create or modify anything. If the user will be deploying workloads, then by all means uncheck this setting to allow unfettered access to the Azure subscription.

With these role-based security concepts in mind, you have the ability to lock down access granularly for each defined role and provide users only with the access they need for your Hyper-V environment in order to complete the task at hand.

Summary

In this chapter, we covered the use case for App Controller. We covered the system requirements, installation, and configuration App Controller. We then connected App Controller to private and public clouds. Finally, we discussed the role-based security model that App Controller pulls from the associated VMM installation.

With these tools, you're now equipped to securely deliver and delegate web-based management of your public and private cloud resources in a granular fashion that is easy to manage and maintain.

As stated earlier, since this book focuses on Hyper-V Security, we did not cover the actual everyday use of App Controller from a cloud management perspective. If you're interested in more information on this topic, Keith Mayer and Yung Chou, both Technical Evangelists with Microsoft, have written a fantastic e-book on App Controller. It can be found at `http://blogs.msdn.com/b/microsoft_press/archive/2013/11/26/free-ebook-microsoft-system-center-cloud-management-with-app-controller.aspx`.

Index

Thank you for buying

Hyper-V Security

About Packt Publishing

Packt, pronounced 'packed', published its first book, *Mastering phpMyAdmin for Effective MySQL Management*, in April 2004, and subsequently continued to specialize in publishing highly focused books on specific technologies and solutions.

Our books and publications share the experiences of your fellow IT professionals in adapting and customizing today's systems, applications, and frameworks. Our solution-based books give you the knowledge and power to customize the software and technologies you're using to get the job done. Packt books are more specific and less general than the IT books you have seen in the past. Our unique business model allows us to bring you more focused information, giving you more of what you need to know, and less of what you don't.

Packt is a modern yet unique publishing company that focuses on producing quality, cutting-edge books for communities of developers, administrators, and newbies alike. For more information, please visit our website at www.packtpub.com.

About Packt Enterprise

In 2010, Packt launched two new brands, Packt Enterprise and Packt Open Source, in order to continue its focus on specialization. This book is part of the Packt Enterprise brand, home to books published on enterprise software – software created by major vendors, including (but not limited to) IBM, Microsoft, and Oracle, often for use in other corporations. Its titles will offer information relevant to a range of users of this software, including administrators, developers, architects, and end users.

Writing for Packt

We welcome all inquiries from people who are interested in authoring. Book proposals should be sent to author@packtpub.com. If your book idea is still at an early stage and you would like to discuss it first before writing a formal book proposal, then please contact us; one of our commissioning editors will get in touch with you.

We're not just looking for published authors; if you have strong technical skills but no writing experience, our experienced editors can help you develop a writing career, or simply get some additional reward for your expertise.

Hyper-V Network Virtualization Cookbook

Hyper-V Network Virtualization Cookbook

ISBN: 978-1-78217-780-7   Paperback: 228 pages

Over 20 recipes to ease the creation of new virtual machines in the networking layer using Hyper-V Network Virtualization

1. Create, configure, and administer System Center 2012 R2 virtual networks with Hyper-V.

2. Design practical solutions to optimize your network solutions.

3. Learn how to control who can access a VM on a specific port to enhance the security of your virtual machine.

Hyper-V Best Practices

Hyper-V Best Practices

ISBN: 978-1-78217-609-1   Paperback: 172 pages

Equip yourselves with the real-world configurations and best practices of Hyper-V to take full advantage of its virtualization capabilities

1. Learn how to deploy standardized Hyper-V solutions quickly and effectively.

2. Leverage all virtualization potential of Hyper-V in production environments.

3. Use state of the art network and storage options with Hyper-V.

Please check **www.PacktPub.com** for information on our titles

Microsoft Hyper-V Cluster Design

ISBN: 978-1-78217-768-5   Paperback: 462 pages

Plan, design, build and maintain Microsoft Hyper-V Server 2012 and 2012 R2 clusters using this essential guide

1. Successfully deploy a Microsoft Hyper-V Server cluster.

2. Use the right tools for building and maintaining a Hyper-V cluster.

3. Master the intricacies of Hyper-V Server in a clustered environment.

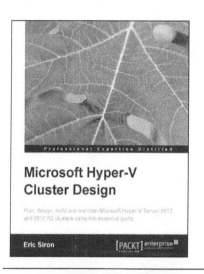

Hyper-V Replica Essentials

ISBN: 978-1-78217-188-1   Paperback: 96 pages

Ensure business continuity and improve your disaster recovery policy using Hyper-V Replica

1. A practical step-by-step guide that goes beyond theory and focuses on giving hands-on experience.

2. Ensure business continuity and faster disaster recovery.

3. Learn how to deploy a failover cluster and encrypt communication traffic.

Please check **www.PacktPub.com** for information on our titles

www.ingramcontent.com/pod-product-compliance
Lightning Source LLC
Chambersburg PA
CBHW082119070326
40690CB00049B/3864